COACH YOUR
Champions

Eric Foley

COACH.YOUR
Champions

The Transformational Giving Approach to Major Donor Fundraising

With
Rebekah Farquhar
and
Amy Karjala

DOERS OF
THE WORD
PUBLISHING

Coach Your Champions:
The Transformational Giving Approach to Major Donor Fundraising

Copyright © 2009 Mission Increase Foundation.
All rights reserved.
Published in the United States by .W Publishing,
a division of Seoul USA, Colorado Springs, Colorado
www.dotheword.org

Edited by: David and Renée Sanford
Cover design: Danielle Kessler
Interior design: Sharon VanLoozenoord

ISBN 978-0-615-39494-7
(previously published under ISBN 978-1-935391-26-5)

Printed in the United States of America

10 9 8 7 6 5 4 3 2

First Edition

Hyun Sook and I dedicate this book
and our work to our children—
Daniel, Christine, Margaret,
Trevor, and Brett
—with the prayer that they will,
through God's unique plan
for each of them,
be transformed into mature champions
of Jesus Christ who Live Life Fully.

Contents

Foreword

I am Josh.

Well, actually, my real name is Greg Stier. But I feel like the main character in this book, Josh Stiller. Although he is fictional, Josh's imaginary composite erupts from real world stories of individuals like me who have to get the privilege of raising money to support their organization cause. As you can see, I'm still learning the vernacular that distinguishes (A) development efforts as a necessary evil required for organizational support from (B) an awe-inspiring catalyst to unite donors for a compelling cause that is just as much theirs as the organization's.

Josh's struggles to break from a dated, unbiblical form of development mirror my own journey in so many ways. He is a character I fully relate to and, most likely, you will too.

As the President of a non-profit organization called Dare 2 Share Ministries, I had received my "training" in development from real world trial and error, from attending a few "how to" seminars, and from interviewing the best development people I could find for their secrets. I spent close to half of my time in the average day doing development related actions (phone calls, letters, donor meetings, preparing for donor meetings, etc.). Yes, I am one of those weird people who actually enjoy raising money for this ministry I so passionately believe in.

I admit now, however, that I didn't know much about the *biblical* art of development before I met Eric Foley a year and a half ago. Sure I knew how to raise money. I was working with a very small team at Dare 2 Share to raise about two million dollars per year to underwrite our evangelism training conferences for teenagers across the nation. I knew how to tell a compelling story about an evangelizing teenager we had trained through one of our conferences, share our ministry need with the donor, and walk away from that meeting with a big fat check. After all, that's the purpose of fundraising, right? Getting donors to pray for and financially support *my* cause?

When I met Eric Foley things began to change big time. In our first meeting I was expecting him to give us better techniques and strategies for raising money. Instead, he began to flip my paradigm of fundraising upside down (or, should I say, right side up?).

I'll never forget Eric sharing the story of Jesus engaging the rich young ruler in Luke 18:17-19. He read the passage, looked up, riveted his eyes on me, and said, "You would have hit the rich young ruler up for a donation, wouldn't you, Greg?" Cringing a bit, I nodded. "But what did Jesus do?" Eric asked, and then said, "He told the young man, 'One thing you lack...'" Eric then went on to expound the importance of ministering to the donor by giving them something valuable, not take something from them (aka "money").

The questions swirling in your mind right now were swirling in mine right then: *Then how in the heck am I supposed to get money for the ministry?* and *What am I supposed to give them beyond our ministry newsletter and a ministry logo-emblazed polo shirt if they give more than a thousand dollars?*

Seeing the internal struggle on my face, Eric answered my non-verbalized objections. For more than an hour he made the case that passionate and persistent financial support of a ministry is a *by-product* of being involved in a compelling cause. In other words, biblical fundraising goes way beyond the donor writing a check. It's them getting involved in the core mission of the organization.

In the year and a half since that original conversation, the Lord has been guiding our board and our team at Dare 2 Share to figure out what our cause is and how to involve everyone as activists in it. In the past eighteen months everything has changed and continues to change. We are moving our organization from a conference ministry to a cause catalyst. Sure, we will still equip teenagers to share their faith through our Dare 2 Share events, but we will seek to engage every one of our donors to join us in this same cause.

Now when I meet with prospective donors my first conversation is not about our need, but how his or her life can be transformed by joining us in this cause of mobilizing teenagers they know to reach their friends for Jesus Christ.

This entire ministry mindset overhaul erupted from that first painful, eye-opening conversation that Eric Foley and I had in my office.

As you read this book you will be confronted with the brutal reality that you have probably been engaged in a form of development that is not only unbiblical, but also largely ineffective. Currently more than 1.6 million non-profit organizations in America are trying to raise money from a constituency reeling from the current global economic crisis. It doesn't take an expert to realize there is going to be less money to spread around to an ever growing number of organizations as we move into the future.

Supporting an organization financially is nice. But these are not nice times. These are lean times. But those organizations that discern their cause and engage their donors to join in it can actually thrive in this economic climate.

This book will help you uncover the core of your cause. It will equip you to prayerfully turn your donors into owners and your partners into activists. Financial support will be the inevitable outcome.

I am Josh. And as you read this book you will discover that you are Josh, too. Read this book, apply its principles, and let's make this radical transformation together. Together, let us pray, discover the core of our cause, engage everyone we can in this cause, and watch how God brings in the money we need to thrive.

Just like the original "Josh" (the biblical one) led his people into the Promised Land, we can, through God's strength, lead everyone connected to our organization into a land flowing with milk and honey.

—*Greg Stier, President, Dare 2 Share Ministries*

Getting Started

It's popular to bash Christians these days for not being more generous. But is that the problem?

"If Christians only gave what they're *supposed* to give," the argument goes, "then every village in Africa could have a well that spews Perrier. And there would be two chaplains for every prisoner in the U.S. and on the moon. Every disease in the universe would now be eradicated, including online viruses. Oh, and we wouldn't have to send out those going-out-of-business-unless-you-give appeal letters to our donors either."

It's interesting that even a relatively tame form of this argument never once crosses Jesus' lips. Or Paul's. Or any of the other New Testament writers. Not once does an inspired apostle groan about what people *should* be giving, but aren't, and how bad that all is, and how much good work is going unaccomplished.

Instead, every story of giving in Scripture—*every* one—is told with an air of respect and holiness and awe, as if something great and paradoxical and wonderful and exciting is invited into being.

Why the difference between our experience and the experience of Jesus and His apostles?

Namely, because Scripture consistently holds up a divine truth about giving that has been completely and bafflingly expunged from the practice of Christian fundraising, namely:

Giving is learned, not latent.

That is, Scripture never portrays giving as something every Christian is automatically ready to do, or ought to do, or will do, if only they're asked the right way, via the right tool or technique or via a direct mail appeal with the right teaser copy and the right size photos. Yet, well over ninety percent of Christian fundraising books and seminars are taught as if giving is indeed latent in Christians, just waiting to be activated by our making an effective case for support.

Instead, whether Scripture teaches about giving time, or money, or jars of oil, or one's modest lunch to feed a huge crowds, there's always a grace-filled gauntlet thrown down in the invitation to give, and that gauntlet is an invitation for the giver to experience a complete transformation.

What the giver accomplishes with his or her gift never garners the Scripture's focus as much as what happens *inside* the giver and those who are a part of the giving process.

The way Scripture pictures it, a person couldn't possibly give without having his or her way of looking at reality—including possessions and who God *really* is—radically changed.

Jesus and the other teachers of generosity in the Bible typically start small, extending invitations to newbies like "Stick out your hand" and "Throw the net out on the other side of the boat" and "Go catch a fish, look in its mouth, take the coin, and then file our 1040's with Rome." These micro-invitations require a suspension of ordinary ways of looking at the world and an extension of radical trust. (Scripture is consistent in contending that both small gifts and recurring gifts require this, by the way.)

If the person complies, the result is unmitigated delight: the one who gives (whether what is given is trust, or lamp oil, or lunch, or a dinner party) ends up with preposterously more-and-different than what he or she started with. There's absolute amazement all the way around and, not infrequently, laughter. No wonder the Scripture tells us, "God loves a cheerful giver."

These entry-level steps into the realm of God's economy open the divine portal to deeper adventures: "Who do you say that I am?" and "I am not commanding you [to give], but I want to test the sincerity of your love by comparing it with the earnestness of others" and "Go, sell all you have, give it to the poor, and then come and follow me."

The adventures change, but the result does not. The one who agrees to run the gauntlet and head a bit further down the rabbit hole of Christian generosity is *forever, fundamentally* changed—in a way that would never accurately be labeled "sacrificial." And, interestingly, the world itself is forever, fundamentally changed, too, when gifts like this are made.

The world is changed not just because the hungry are fed and the captives set free (though that's not a bad start), but also because our ways of thinking about security and importance and practicality are upended.

But let me show you a more excellent way still . . .

"Go into all nations, baptizing and teaching" and "And the things you have heard me say in the presence of many witnesses entrust to reliable men who will also be qualified to teach others" and "It is enough for the student to be like his teacher, and the servant like his master."

The initiation into the mystery progresses from *imitation* to *replication*. (And if these Scriptures don't seem like fundraising verses to you, you picked up the right book.)

And the movement toward Transformational Giving spreads! Such fundraising, incidentally, is the fastest way to spread a social cause.

If this process of comprehensively teaching how to give saturates the New Testament, though, why is it so weirdly *absent* from the way churches and Christian nonprofits do fundraising? Why, in other words, do churches brag about not taking offerings while announcing to first-time visitors to put away their wallets? Why do Christian nonprofits gravitate to systems of "friend-raising" or to hit-and-run fundraising events designed to make the ask as quickly and painlessly as possible?

If giving is something we should be teaching, why is it so painful to ask and why aren't people learning to give?

That is why I wrote this book.

The fundraising agenda for churches and Christian ministries has for way too many years been dominated by the thinking of secular nonprofits, for whom fundraising has always been an arm-twisting, necessary evil.

It's time for a fresh look at giving and asking, and time to change the way we fundraise.

This book presents a whole new way to look at major donors— true major donors. After all, every organization needs them, but how in the world can we find them and ever get them to give?

In this book, I will show you that your major donors are more ready and able to give than ever before, whether the economy is up or down. Interestingly, they really aren't all that stingy. And they are especially ready for you to give them a greater gift than they give to you.

This book is intended as an intensely practical and detailed major donor development manual that will help you step by step to revamp your approach to fundraising.

"That's funny," you may be thinking. "It sure looks a lot like a fiction story without a lot of bullet points and stuff."

And indeed that's true. That's because the first thing to go when we revamp our approach to fundraising is our reliance on tools and techniques to bring us success. You can almost read Jesus' entire ministry as a rebuke to those religious leaders who attempted to turn the Hebrew Scriptures into a lockdown series of tools and techniques—and who ended up locking God out in the process. "You diligently study the Scriptures because you think that by them you possess eternal life," sighs an exasperated Jesus in John 5:39-40. "These are the Scriptures that testify about me, yet you refuse to come to me to have life."

In other words, the Scriptures aren't merely an instruction book. They're a road map that, when you become a doer of the word and not just a hearer only, put you on a collision course with a radically, exuberantly abundant life that goes by the name of Jesus. Systematize things by knocking the story out of it and it's like cracking the peanut open, throwing the nut away, and eating the shell.

Translation for fundraising purposes:

Your fundraising doesn't need a *different* set of tools and techniques. Your fundraising program needs an encounter with the living God—daily. A 1-2-3 to-do list in outline form is not an encounter with the living God. Often, frankly, it's a way to avoid having an encounter with the living God.

And that's why this book is written as a story. It's a story about a Christian nonprofit probably not dissimilar from yours, doing great work and hating fundraising—doing enough of it (far, far more than the executive director would like) to stay in business, barely, and feeling so yucky about it all that showering after a donor call doesn't seem like such a bad idea.

You'll notice that the book is intensely committed to realism: the ministry stumbles and fumbles not only forward into a new way of thinking about fundraising, but backward as well. As Jesus' own disciples illustrate, that's the nature of authentic discipleship. You may be able to master tools and techniques, but when it comes to Transformational Giving, you can't master God and the hand He deals you. So you'll lurch forward *and* backward in this great learning journey—and the message of this book is: That's okay. There's no other way to do it.

But this book is also intensely hopeful. As long as God stays faithful to His character, doing the Word will always yield a better Kingdom harvest than doing the Secular Fundraising Square Dance Fandango. There's no doubt a learning adventure awaits you as you leave the old ways behind and press ahead. Guaranteed, you and your organization *will* be changed and challenged radically along the way.

But God will provide as you do the Word: no matter what those secular fundraising voices in your brain keep screaming, the truth is you already have as many major donors as you need to do fully everything that God is calling you to do. (Remember, however, that giving is learned, not latent. You have some discipling to do. Your donors are going to learn to provide for your shared cause at the same time you're learning to practice Transformational Giving. In fact, they're probably going to learn a lot from and through your own learning process, which is likely to occur in stumbling and fumbling steps in equal parts forward and backward.)

It's virtually guaranteed that you'll enjoy coaching champions infinitely more than you ever liked soliciting donors. Your donors (now champions) will, too, and they'll tell you so to your face before the adventure unfolds too many pages.

And speaking of not many pages, I'll be back at the close of the story to highlight the transformational steps you and your fundraising program will experience as you stop soliciting major donors and instead start coaching champions.

In the meantime, we'd better hurry over to the office of Live Life Fully. The executive director is just arriving after his most recent attempt to solicit a financial gift from a major donor prospect (through a compelling presentation of need and opportunity, of course).

I wonder how that Secular Fundraising Square Dance Fandango is working for him?

Chapter 1

I could have been a dishonest car salesman if I wanted extortion as a career, Josh thought to himself as he returned from a failed potential major donor meeting. *I know I'm supposed to be in youth ministry, and I know this is where God wants me, but fundraising? Isn't there another way I can find money for Live Life Fully?*

Josh drove his car into the gravel driveway of Live Life Fully's office. Situated in a gray, ten-year-old portable behind a church, the office was three blocks from the highest crime neighborhood in Portland. Even as he stepped out of his car, another drug deal was happening across the street. "Even if we run out of money, we'll never run out of teens," he mumbled. Not a day went by without some form of drug dealing or gang-related violence—usually involving minors—near the office.

The squat, nondescript portable attracted little attention from those who weren't looking for it, but to Josh that was a definite plus—his small staff only had to paint over graffiti and replace broken windows every few months.

The church itself was small and resembled a cement fortress. Its sole distinguishing feature was a weather-beaten message board whose ransom note-like letters presently were arrayed to read, "Autumn leaves, but Jesus loves." Colorful graffiti had taken over the adornment function once held by stained glass windows that had long since been replaced by crusty plastic. The cement looked as Spartan and functional as the day it had been laid seventy years ago.

Josh had never had much use for nice cars or fancy offices. To effectively minister to the kids in the neighborhood, he had even moved his family there when he founded the ministry. With his primary source of income more a seasonal creek than steady stream, his wife, Beth, had to return to work part-time in order to make ends meet. His three children, just finishing elementary school when they moved in ten years ago, were now accustomed to hearing gunshots at night and passing through the metal detector on the way into school.

Despite the transition troubles, no one could deny the fact that God had gifted Josh and his family for this line of work. A former youth counselor and pastor, he had a natural ease with teens. He and Beth had managed to raise a family unfazed by the urban blight. What was once a crazy longing for him became his daily work when he founded LLF.

For Josh, gunshots were manageable.

Fundraising, on the other hand, was like dying a slow and painful death. Month after month.

Josh figured he should have been eligible for combat pay while living and working in the neighborhood. He made weekly visits to the nearest juvenile detention centers, trying to steer his young neighbors away from their seemingly inevitable future. Sometimes he would become acutely aware that he was fighting a losing battle. But he never doubted it was a losing battle: he would never give up fighting.

One of LLF's current staff members, Azariah, was a teen rescued from the street culture and gang life. Josh met him shortly after Azariah made his first and last visit to juvenile detention. Scared and mostly alone—except for an abusive, drug-addicted mother—his life pleaded for a mentor. Josh volunteered for the role, mentoring Azariah into Moody Bible Institute and—to everyone's surprise, including Josh's—back, where he now acted as the yang to Josh's yin on the staff of LLF.

It was hardly lucrative work. Josh and Azariah and the volunteers tried to mimic any and all fundraising methods they saw other ministries doing in an effort to keep the doors of their little portable open. Bake sales, auctions, church dinners, and the occasional support letter comprised most of their income streams.

During financially desperate months, such as the summer they were now enduring, Josh would make personal calls to people he knew in an attempt to raise money. More often than not, it consisted of calling friends with semi-desperate pleas to meet the budget or make payroll.

Like the lunch from which he was just returning; empty handed save for the receipt from picking up the check.

Josh shook his head and got out of the car, ignoring the returned donor proposal on his dashboard.

Funds seem to appear miraculously for other ministries, thought Josh. *How do they find the big donors? They all have rich people on their boards and at their fundraising events, and they get full-time fundraising staff so their directors can focus on real ministry. How do I get in on that deal? And how do I get in on those donors?* Nonprofit it was. The expression on Josh's face communicated his most recent funding failure to the two folks in the portable. The front room of the building functioned as the reception area and potential donor meeting room. He and staff and volunteers had set up offices in one of the two rooms in the back, leaving the other room open for youth counseling and other LLF programs. *The real ministry I hardly get to do anymore*, thought Josh resentfully.

His hip buzzed, and he reflexively pulled out his cell phone and thumbed a text reply to a teen he used to mentor. This gave him a way to divert his gaze as he walked through the reception area and into his office, avoiding the volunteer stuffing envelopes with his latest newsletter. *Lois*, he mused. *Looks like she wants to talk.* He chuckled to himself. *Eagerness to talk to me is inversely proportional to one's financial resources.*

Azariah glanced up from the financial spreadsheet as Josh entered. Though finances were not Azariah's strong point, he was definitely better than Josh with the books. *Actually, I wouldn't mind working the spreadsheet*, Josh mused. *It beats looking at a donor, hinting around about bankruptcy, and then watching them change the subject.*

Azariah waited for Josh to situate himself at his desk before asking, "Are we in the black, chief?"

Josh slouched back in his chair and took off his tie. "Red, Azariah, is the new black. Mr. Andrew Jones passed on the deal of the century to keep us solvent. To quote, 'Josh, the work you do is amazing. I could certainly never do it myself.' Translation: 'And I'm not going to fund it, either.' I hinted and hinted to him how we needed money. I even asked him to pray with me for funds. He just changed the subject and stiffed me with the bill. What do I have to do, beg these people for money outright?"

"Try a stickup—works well in this neighborhood." Azariah started laughing.

"Azzie, donors should *love* us—we keep kids away from their car windows. A donation to us is a half-way decent investment. Then again . . ." Josh took off his tie and rolled it into a ball before pitching it at the plastic basketball hoop on the wall. "None of these donors want to talk about finances. Jones was what, my fifth strikeout in a row?" *It's so awkward.* Josh shook his head, trying to dispel the discouraging train of thought. "Where are we going wrong?"

"Maybe we just need new friends. Who do we know that has a truck full of extra cash lying around and needs to unload it?"

"New friends? More lunches?" Josh shook his head. "That won't work. It hasn't worked. Just more people saying no. *They* know I'm after their money, and *I* know I'm after their money. It's a perfect stalemate." He paused for breath, but the look on his face convinced Azariah not to interrupt the silence. "Yeah, having a few more rich friends on a diet would be nice. Or maybe a few people who want to leave us in their wills."

"Do you plan on scheduling their deaths around your funding needs?"

Josh stopped to ponder the thought. "CSI guys always seem to catch on. And, anyway, we need money quickly. Donor deaths will just have to wait."

Azariah opened a long Excel spreadsheet and turned his monitor toward Josh. "Behold, your donor file. Might I suggest calling a few of these?"

"Those are just regular donors. Newsletter people. We need newspaper *owners*. Rich Christians called by God to give away all their money to obscure youth ministries. A few rich people—they could give more than all those newsletter folks combined." Josh took off his suit coat and rolled up the sleeves of his shirt. "Speaking of which, I should go stuff said newsletters."

"Yeah—and Lois wants to talk to you about next week's bake sale, too." Azariah handed him a thick folder marked with a hand-written *bake sale* label. "They need a few more people to bring cookies, and it sounds like promotional things aren't going too well."

"Problems with the bake sale!" moaned Josh, reluctantly accepting the folder. "We can't even acquire cookie donors!"

I should do this cheerfully, he chided himself. *Lois is a faithful volunteer. She's trying her best. I really shouldn't take out my frustration about donors on the poor woman.* He forced himself to smile as he strode back to the reception area. "Lois, how's it going?"

The grandmother of a teen converted through Josh's work, Lois had been faithfully giving from her fixed income for several years. Her grandson, T.J., like the other teens in the neighborhood, was on the fast track to a life of crime. He ended up in juvenile detention after a drug deal gone awry. Following a probation officer's recommendation, Lois came to Josh, begging him to keep her grandson from following the rest of his friends into jail. Josh spent three years mentoring T.J, seeing him off to college and later officiating his wedding.

For Lois, the newsletters and the bake sales were her babies. She ran them faithfully every year, doing her best to keep LLF alive and on the streets reaching teens.

"Going just fine, Josh. Did I hear you and Azzie talking about money troubles?"

Josh kept focusing on the newsletters below him. *What did she hear?* He kept a straight face and even tone of voice as he responded. "Oh, just the usual. Summertime's tough. Everyone loves the ministry, but no one wants to fund us—at least not with serious funding. Just a few big donors could keep this ministry going."

"Oh. I see." Lois steadily continued to stuff newsletters. "Well, maybe this newsletter will end up reaching a few rich donors. I really like how you did this one—one of your best yet."

He continued staring at the newsletters, pondering how to respond. "Well, Lois," he began slowly, "it doesn't quite work like that. The bigger donors get angry if you send them mail, so we don't send them any. They want, you know, the personal treatment."

"I can see how that works."

Lois quietly kept folding the letters for a few minutes.

"Josh," she said at last. "How are your kids?"

"They're doing great." He nodded, happy the subject seemed to be changing. *Youth! Finally a subject I'm actually competent in.* "Lauren, our oldest, just started college this year."

"That's nice. I put three of my seven kids through college, once upon a time. Schools were cheaper then. It's too bad the rest of the kids never wanted to go." She tapped a thin envelope on the table. "Josh, how do you feel about favoritism between your kids?"

Josh frowned as he pondered the thought. *Favoritism? What is she getting at? Does she feel guilty that some of her kids went to college and the others didn't?* "Well, I mean, it's obviously a bad thing, Lois. But something tells me that's not what you mean."

"Do you favor one of you children over the others?"

"Favor? Oh, no," Josh said, easing up. "I think all parents try to work to be fair. Besides, God says he hates favoritism."

"I thought so. It's somewhere in James, isn't it?" She stopped tapping the envelope, staring intently at Josh. "Do you think it relates to donors?"

So much for a non-fundraising conversation, sighed Josh. "Lois, it's different in fundraising. We're not showing favoritism between donors. We just need to be good stewards of our time, so we spend the most time with the ones who have the potential to make big gifts. The major donors tend to, you know, need more attention."

"So you give them the attention they want to get the money you want? That sounds like a fair trade." Both silently continued to stuff the envelopes.

Lois finally broke the silence.

"Josh, what exactly is a major donor? Do I know any of the major donors here?"

"Well, technically I can't really share financial information . . ." hesitated Josh. "But, come to think of it, even if I could, there wouldn't be anything to share. I guess that pretty much answers your question, huh?"

She nodded knowingly. "So a major donor is one who has a lot of money, and gives a lot of money?"

Josh stopped stuffing the envelopes. "Well, it's not *just* about the numbers, but I can tell you this: If we don't get a number of major donors soon, the unemployment number in Portland will go up by at least one."

"It can't come to that." She shook her head. "That just doesn't seem right. I wonder how Jesus would raise money. I can't think of any fundraising stories in the Bible exactly, but there is this story about a widow and two mites. Does that ring a bell?"

He avoided her intense stare. "Yeah, it's right after the story of the widow who ran a bake sale for a nearly bankrupt nonprofit." He looked at his watch. "And speaking of bake sale, Azariah said that you had something you needed to talk about?" *No one could be more serious about a bake sale than her*, thought Josh.

"Well," harrumphed Lois, "We have twenty-seven ladies from the church bringing cookies, but the promotional flyers went out late. Mary Ellen said that her computer would speed things up, but I don't think she knows how to use it—she tried to use a fancy flyer making program, but the handmade ones we've always used look just as good, and the computer took twice as long. We aren't sure how big of a crowd we'll have." She shrugged. "Even if Mary Ellen can't make flyers quickly, she can make a mean batch of scotchmellows."

"You know," continued Lois, "this would just be so much easier if major donor didn't have to mean money. Mary Ellen could be your major cookie baker, I could be your major newsletter stuffer and bake sale organizer, and I'm sure we could get other people to be the major cookie eaters."

Josh smiled sadly. "Right now, I don't know what a major donor is. I just know that we don't have any, and if we don't find any soon, we'll be paying our staff with scotchmellow cookies." Josh picked up all of the stuffed envelopes and placed them in a haphazard stack. "You happen to know any good no-cost, high yield fundraising ideas we can implement in the next week?"

"Quite a few, Josh. All of them bad. How many do you want to hear?"

"Just one," he mumbled. "Whichever one will get us out of this mess. What do you have? It couldn't be any worse than the brush-off I received today from a major donor—a major *non*-donor—when I told him we needed money to make budget."

She nodded sympathetically. For a moment, to Josh she looked quite wise. She responded gently and deliberately, like a grandmother teaching a grandchild something difficult but important. "Josh, telling a donor that you need his money—that you'll cease to exist as an organization without his money—isn't actually a very effective way to raise money, no matter how sincerely it's said." Lois frowned thoughtfully. "Josh, maybe people don't want to just help your ministry. They want to help these kids."

"But isn't that what I'm begging them to do, Lois?" groaned Josh. "When they support the ministry, they're supporting me working with these kids."

"Yes, supporting the kids, but maybe they want something more. Maybe people are like me—wanting to help, but really not sure what to do."

"People these days don't want to just give the money and sit on the sidelines. Maybe they don't trust people the way they used to. I don't know. But maybe there's something more," Josh confessed.

"That something more is why I'm here, you know. I want to give what I can, but I also want to be in the starting lineup. I don't pay you so I can sit in the stands and cheer. You shouldn't even let me do that if I wanted to. I don't give you money to help you run your organization. I give money *to reach teens*. I volunteer *to reach teens*. I want to do ministry *with* you, not watch you. I want to see more lives changed the way my grandson's life was changed."

Josh thought for several moments before responding. "I've never had anyone tell me that before. I've never even thought of that. Lois, you're a very special donor."

"A major donor?" she asked coyly.

"Um . . ." he sighed. "Now I'm really confused. You're a *better* donor than other donors, but . . . well, I've always been told that major donors give lots of money. On top of that, if what you're saying is true, then my donors may not even really care about LLF. Maybe they like the kids, but I don't see them selling their homes in Westside suburbia to come over here and help the teens they're supposed to love so much."

"Fact of life, Josh," she said. "If you're focused on LLF, you're looking for people who want to fund your ministry." She emphasized the "your," even raising her eyebrows at him. "You'll miss out on meeting more people like me. As much as we like you, our focus is helping kids like T.J. and Azzie get back on track."

Josh pulled out his newsletter from one of the envelopes, reading it to himself. He sighed. "How would you even make a newsletter focus on kids without focusing on the organization? If you focus just on kids, maybe people won't give to us. Maybe they'll just go do the work themselves." *That's a scary thought,* mused Josh, half surprised that he found himself thinking that way.

Azariah opened the door. "Josh, you have a phone call from Richard at Juvie. He says he has a kid who wants to talk to you."

Josh excused himself quickly. He always had one more teen to reach, one more juvenile detention visit to make. "No time for fundraising," he said to Lois. "Duty calls yet again. I'm back to my real job of helping kids."

Azariah sat quietly, sending off the last of the receipt letters for the month to donors as he waited for Josh to finish the call. After a brief minute or two, Josh replaced the receiver on the phone.

"Sounds like you had a fun conversation, dude."

"Fun?" He rubbed the bald spot on his 40-year old head. "My head is spinning, and I'm not sure if it should be. How could a seventy-year-old lady mess up my entire categories of fundraising when we were talking about scotchmellow cookies?"

"Scotchmellow cookies are the best . . . chocolate chips, caramels, marshmallows, and graham crackers? That would make my head spin," Azzie teased.

Josh shook his head. "She's been messing with me since she first started volunteering—encouraging me to recruit more volunteers, organizing bake sale after bake sale, sending every extended family member in for some reason or another. I think she's related to half of our volunteers."

"She's the best street-level staff member you have, and she's a volunteer. You should try to find more individuals like Lois. Her initials are even LLF, just like this organization. That's built-in marketing, man."

"Azzie, you're not helping. The fact that Lois is the best is part of my problem. She's asking questions about fundraising now—I've been doing this for ten years, but in five minutes she's challenged my definition of a major donor, and I'm not sure she's wrong."

Then again, she's never sat across from Mr. Andrew Jones at lunch, thought Josh. *You have to work with them the way they want to work with you. If that means a yearly check at a yearly lunch meeting, hold the newsletters—that's what they get. If they want to volunteer, that's their deal.*

"I thought I heard her say that she might be a major donor?" Azzie ventured. "You think she may be thinking about putting you in her will or something?"

"All the cookies in her estate," mumbled Josh absent-mindedly as he reached for the Bible on the corner of his desk. "You just said she was our best staff member—does that make her a major donor, even though she gives only $10 a month?" Josh flipped through the second half of the ragged book. "She reminded me about the parable of the widows and mites. Where do I find the widow and the mites?"

"Any house on this street, man. Dust mites, termites—"

"Azzie," he interrupted, "Widow and mites. Where would I find it?"

"Luke 21 and Mark 12." Azariah grinned proudly. "I always knew Bible college was good for something."

Josh read the passages to himself, rubbing his temples as he tried to process Lois's ideas. "How does this relate to fundraising? And how could the widow give more? She gave . . ."

"The equivalent to $10 a month?" Azariah offered.

"Yeah, but Jesus said she gave more than all of them." Josh reread the passage, trying to straighten his thoughts. *This isn't about fundraising. Nobody asked her to give everything. She just gave. Fundraising is about getting people to give who don't want to, isn't it?*

"Maybe the point of the story is that you don't have to give a lot . . . to give a lot, or something." Now Azzie was scratching his head. "So was Lois right? Does major donor have less to do with the sum of money and more to do with . . . I dunno, something else?"

"It sounds nice, but you can't run a business like that. You can't even run a nonprofit—or you'll be a literal *non*profit."

That widow wasn't the one keeping the temple open, thought Josh. *She just had a lot of faith when she gave. We have those. What we don't have are the people to keep* us *open. For that, I think you may need to have a Pharisee or two.*

"What 'something else' could define major donors?" Josh asked, not sure if he was directing his question to the Bible, Azzie, or maybe even Lois in the next room. "We can't go around figuring out who gave what percentage of his or her income. Even if we did, it would take a whole neighborhood of widows."

"That might beat major donor meetings," Azzie said, pointing to Josh's rumpled tie on the floor.

"Hardly," Josh challenged. "Weighing motives? Jesus can do that, but I'm not psychic—I have a hard enough time just figuring out how to ask people for money."

Besides, it just isn't practical, complained Josh to himself. *Sure, it's great that the widow had such deep faith, but two mites plus two mites plus two mites doesn't equal an operating budget.*

He stared at the page, trying to see a deeper meaning in the text. "Do you think it has anything to do with being cause-focused instead of organization-focused?"

Azzie imitated Josh rubbing his head, instead rubbing his curly black hair. "Cause-focused? I missed that part."

"Lois said that people work with us and give to us not because they want to support us, but because they like to help teens."

He nodded. "I heard some guy talk about something like that in one of my personal support classes at Moody. He said fundraising was changing . . . letters couldn't be me-focused, or something like that. I wasn't really listening all that much, but it sounds cool now."

"I don't suppose you took notes." Josh finally got up from his chair and pulled out a 4'x6' white board from behind his desk. "I need to think about this."

Azariah opened the window and fanned the air as Josh broke out the dry-erase pens. "Maybe you could think when I'm not around, man."

"I need you to think with me. What would happen if we were cause-focused in fundraising? What would change?" *What does that even mean?*

Josh scribbled "cause-focused" and "organization-focused" on the board. "If we were cause-focused, how would we look? Or how do we look now?"

Azariah started counting on his fingers. "*We* send newsletters telling donors what great work *we* do so they can send *us* money so *we* can keep doing our great work. *We* hold bake sales and convince major donors to give . . . or not . . . after a round of golf and a nice get-to-know-you lunch where *we* foot the tab."

"And we can assume that all of those go under 'organization-focused' ... I think." Josh jotted down the list on the white board. "Now Lois said she worked with us because she wanted to help teens. If we take her as an example of a good donor ... maybe

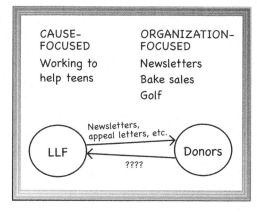

a major donor, depending on what a major donor is ... what is 'cause-focused'?"

"Working to help teens, not us."

Josh wrote that on the board. "That's the beginning of it. Then what?"

Azariah sat back in his chair. "I feel like I'm back in school. How about I write and you come up with some answers?"

"My handwriting is more legible, and you don't like the smell of deep thought." Josh doodled a smiley face with the tongue out in the corner of the whiteboard. *That's how I feel about fundraising.* "What about the last newsletter? Was it cause-focused?"

"Not exactly. You talked about LLF ... how it grew, what we did, how we were doing, what you thought of the growth, and why they should send you money."

"What if it was cause-focused? How would it change?"

"We wouldn't send it."

Josh stopped writing. "No newsletter? How would we communicate to donors?"

"We could have newsletters, but they wouldn't be like *that* one," mused Azariah. "We wouldn't have sent that one. We would send something about ... I dunno. Maybe how they could do what we do with teens they know? Warning signs of drug use? Support and encouragement if they've got an Azzie in their life?"

"That's a scary thought. Doing what we do?" Josh wrote it down and capped his pen. "What about donor relationships? How do we talk to donors now and how would it be different?"

"All the world's a stage," Azzie quoted. "The donors are all watching us. We tell them about us, they throw us money instead of roses."

"We send them a letter, they respond to us. What is that . . ." Josh drew a circle for the organization and a circle for the donors, with an arrow going in between the two. "A two-way street?"

"One way freight train, more like," Azariah crossed his arms thoughtfully. "We do all the talking. Nobody's sending *us* letters, man, unless they say, 'Take me off your mailing list.' It's like having a cell phone that only calls out. We don't get any calls in, and we don't even know who's listening—if anybody's listening at all."

"Has to be some way to fix that." Josh capped his pen. "I think these pens are starting to get to my head. What you just said shouldn't make that much sense, but it does. Lois said she wants to do this ministry as much as we do. She gives because of our cause."

"Well, maybe there are others like her? How do we find them?"

Josh shrugged his shoulders. "I have no idea. All I know how to do is our 'one way' communication, and if we stop that, then we'll really be in trouble."

"Josh, maybe you could try adding some two ways into the mix— just to see what happens. Look at today's conversation with Lois. That wasn't one way—she's about as passionate as us when it comes to this cause. Maybe we just need to have two-way conversations with all of our donors."

"All of our donors?" Josh's eyebrows arched. "Talking with Lois was exhausting enough. How could I do this for all of our donors?"

Azzie stared at Josh for a moment. "Josh, 'all our donors'? Even if you could get appointments with 'all' our donors, we don't have enough to fill a day of appointments. We might not even have anyone answer the phone, man."

"No, we have to have people listening." Josh wagged the pen at Azariah. "Lois is, and the people I talk to seem to like us. What if donors really are as passionate about this cause as Lois is?"

"And the point of all these donors being connected to us is . . . what? We do all the work and end up with six dozen leftover cookies."

"We need to find people who share our connection. How do we find people with two mites, or two hundred mites, that they really want to share, who want to share our cause?"

"How did you find Lois?"

Josh paused. *How long ago did we find Lois?* "She found us. She wanted to get involved . . . see her grandson get help. I just happened to be in the wrong place at the wrong time."

Azzie nodded. "Flyers at Juvie: 'Donate to LLF.'"

"Azzie, not quite like that . . . but then again, that might work. We don't have to make having a kid on drugs a requirement, but people may be able to do like Lois did. She found us because she shared our cause—helping teens. It was our shared cause," Josh said, rubbing his stubbly chin. "She didn't sit back and watch us work. She's here stuffing newsletters. She is passionate enough about it to do something and get involved. You want to get parents with kids on drugs? I know half a dozen already who are passionate about getting their kids off drugs—just like Lois, and you, and me. These parents care for their kids, and the community wants to get help for their kids." Josh drew a series of little circles all over the board. "I think we need to have a two-way conversation with all of these people."

"Great idea, boss. But I don't see a line forming outside *this* building."

"I don't want a bunch of people here in the office—even if they fit, I wouldn't know what to do with them . . ." Josh scratched his head with a capped pen. "But there has to be some connection between passion, cause, and fundraising. These people are living the cause—more than we are. They are passionate, because these are *their* kids, in *their* neighborhoods, in *their* homes. Of course they want to see some of these kids off their streets. It's their ministry as much as it is ours."

"Okay, that makes sense . . . except that if it's *their* ministry, why would they give to *us*?" Azariah asked, palms turned up. "We should be giving to them then, right?"

"If they were giving to us, I would halfway think about that." *But they're not giving to us*, Josh thought. *Lois gives, but not much. Maybe . . .* "What if it isn't about the money?" Josh continued. "I mean, Lois gives $10 a month. She knows as well as we do that it won't make much of a difference. We have wanted major donors to give so they can watch us fix the problem. But she wants to get involved and fix the problem—whether she has enough money to or not."

Azzie sat on the edge of his desk with his arms crossed. "Josh, where are you going with this?"

"She's . . . I think she's more blessed by giving through us than by receiving news of our great work." He frowned. "I think I just totaled my model of fundraising."

"Yeah, you did," nodded Azariah. "I even heard at a certain Bible Institute I attended that we are all ambassadors of the gospel, which would mean that the donors are supposed to be doing this ministry. Do they get to opt out of ministry when they give?"

"Nope. They give . . . *through* the ministry, not to it. They give to us, but they could do like Lois does . . . serve through us while they're at it. If that's the case, we need to start talking to them, and letting them talk to us—making this a two-way network."

Azzie shook his head hesitantly. "Maybe a two-way network . . . but something more than that. If these donors are serving the same cause, don't you think they need to talk to more people than just us? Set them up with Lois, man. And each other. We could create some sort of network, and hopefully they talk about more than the latest neighborhood gossip."

"So a two-way network, except with a little multiplication?"

Azzie took the pen, wrote *bake sale* on the board, and started scrambling the arrows. "So, we have a bake sale network? In this network we have donors talking to donors . . . talking to people about us . . . who talk to more donors . . . and they just come to us when they need something."

"That's cool." Josh put a star next to Azzie's drawing.

"What other networks do we have?" Josh asked.

"Not many. We have a group that focuses on mentoring kids. And that 24-hour hotline group. Maybe a few others."

"So how can we impact those networks, and maybe even create some new ones?"

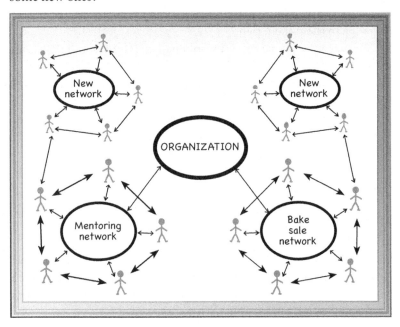

Azzie started drawing more circles representing more donors in more networks and put a label over each unique group. "Dude, you are scrambling my brain. I can't even draw all these networks. How can we manage them? This looks more like ... scribbled networks or spaghetti than ministry."

"Yeah, but think of all the people we could reach with one or two networks—if one person talks to two people, then they talk to four people, who then talk to eight people ... which means sixteen people ... this is amazing! If we can get them to talk to us and to each other, we would have the most powerful donor connection ever!"

"If the donors are all working to do our jobs, and they are talking to each other," Azzie continued, "then we aren't the focus—we're more the director, or the stage, or maybe even the audience."

"Or the cheerleaders."

Azzie put up one finger. "The donors can be actors in a tale of sound and fury ... the tale of youth work. All the world is a stage—so let's start putting out actors."

"Azzie, enough with the Shakespeare. Bible college students don't usually study Shakespeare in their free time."

Azzie took the pen and drew a stage picture under *cause-focused* and added a few stick fig-ure actors. "But what does that do to our fundraising? Directors pay actors, not the other way around."

"Yes ..." *Dead end,* thought Josh. *Maybe this idea wasn't so good after all.*

"Maybe ..." Azariah poked the board with the pen. "If they really share our cause and carry the

message to their networks, then fundraising will happen through them more than through us. Maybe fundraising wouldn't be our job anymore."

"I like that dream, but what happens when we wake up?" Josh sighed. "Lois tells her friends to give ... which equals $30 per month instead of $10 per month. She'll do that, but will other people? It's hard to ask for money. We're professional-ish and we can't even ask for money. How do we get a bunch of amateur networks to ask for money?"

"That's part of networks, man," Azariah replied. "It's not like we coach them to ask for money. Maybe it's like seeing a sunset—if you're excited about it, you want all your friends to share your experience. If you give and get involved, and it's amazing, you'll want all your friends to give. You won't walk around asking people—you'll just share the glow, and people will follow you to the window to watch the next one."

"If that was working now, I'd say it was brilliant." Josh plopped back in his chair. "As it is, we have a bake sale happening in a few days. What do we tell them to do? Ask for money because the cookies are so good?"

"Okay . . . that doesn't work—but is that our fault or their fault?" Azariah sat on the corner of Josh's desk. "I mean, we gave them a bake sale to do, and now it's a dead end. Maybe we need to tell them to do different things. Because 'Hey, come to a bake sale' is definitely organization-focused. You can't tell the cause from the cookies, man."

Josh shook his head. "What a can of worms Lois opened."

Azzie folded his arms and grinned as he surveyed the white board. "Dude, I think this is going to change us . . . maybe even change us a lot. That's kinda cool."

Josh shook his head, finally giving in to Azariah's Shakespeare obsession. "Methinks the lady doth protest too much."

The two drifted back into their work, with the whiteboard sitting in the room like an awkward guest. Azariah left the office a few hours later to meet with a small group of teens just out of juvenile detention and on probation. Josh stayed behind, cleaning up the last of the day's work.

What a day, he mused. *One sour donor meeting, one bake sale trying to flop, and . . . and my entire major donor model up in smoke. Lois, what have you done?*

He pulled a legal pad out of his desk, hoping to process the various puzzle pieces that were trying to become a coherent picture in his mind. *Donors talk to each other. We help the donors network. We work with the donors to get them involved with the cause, not our organization—with something more than giving. The donors talk to us, and network with each other—one gigantic, tangled web.* He stopped writing and fiddled with his pencil for several moments before writing down his final thought.

What if the relationship between donors is as important as the relationship between the donor and our ministry?

Josh stared at the question that had materialized on his legal pad. *Did I just write that? Do I mean that?*

He stood and hesitantly erased the jumbled mass of letters and arrows from the whiteboard.

Question of the Moment, he wrote at the top. Below that he wrote, *What if the relationship between donors is as important as the relationship between the donor and our ministry?*

He capped the pen, shut down the laptop, and left for home.

QUESTION OF THE MOMENT

1. What if the relationship between donors is as important as the relationship between the donor and our ministry?

To Ponder

1. Do you have any volunteers like Lois working with you in your ministry? What have you done to train and equip those individuals to do more for your cause? Have you equipped them to do what *they* sense they should be doing for the cause? Have you helped them figure this out for themselves? Or have you caused them to adopt your answer to the question?

2. How do you apply the "don't show favoritism" admonition in James to your fundraising efforts?

3. Are your donor communications focused on your organization or your cause? What activities or communications does your ministry have that are organization-focused? Cause-focused? How do you know? How would your donors (especially your donors like Lois) answer this question?

4. What does the story of the widow's mite say about how you should raise money for your ministry?

5. Has your focus on acquiring high-net worth donors caused you to miss opportunities to spread your cause broadly through multiple donor networks?

Chapter 2

Josh's stomach tightened when he saw Lois's car in the lot as he pulled in the following Monday morning. *What is she doing here? We don't have any more newsletters to send.* Lois and Azzie came out of the office a moment later. Each grabbed two trays of cookies, stacked them carefully, and walked slowly back into the building. *Ah . . . the bake sale. Am I going to have six dozen leftover scotchmellow cookies in my office?* He subconsciously patted his midsection and resolved not to eat six dozen cookies . . . maybe just one. He reluctantly got out of the car, grabbed a tray of cookies himself, and meandered into the office. "Good morning, Azzie. Lois." Josh glared at the carnage of cookies all over his desk, then shook his head and sighed. "Am I supposed to eat all of these?"

Azzie grinned and shrugged, taking another bite of a partially eaten snickerdoodle cookie. "Don't know, but I can help. Lois said there were about ten dozen cookies left over, but we don't have space in the lobby since we have the teen dads support group meeting here at three."

Josh emphatically moved a tray off his desk and back into the lobby. "Yes, we do. The teen dads always try to empty the candy dish— this time they can empty trays of cookies. Might as well get some use out of them. Did we break $200?"

Azzie shrugged again, moving towards the door. "I'm getting more cookies. Ask Lois."

That means no, Josh thought. *What am I going to do with this mess? Last time it was six dozen cookies. Now it's ten? This just keeps getting worse. Why can't volunteers run a cookie sale? Maybe they should stick to stuffing letters.*

Lois came in with a tray of coconut and chocolate drop cookies, leaving them next to the tray Josh had already evicted from his office. She attempted to smile enthusiastically. "Azzie said the teen dads are coming today. I'm sure they like cookies."

"I'm sure they do, too, Lois. Still, that's a lot of left over cookies. How many did we sell?" Lois's smile lessened a bit. *This is bad. Brace for impact.*

"We sold random cookies here and there, but I think the Girl Scouts beat us to the neighborhood."

Josh tried to laugh at her humor. "As if the Girl Scouts could survive in this neighborhood. Didn't the last Girl Scouts in here get their entire wagon of cookies stolen?"

"Yes, so in comparison, our bake sale did amazingly well." Lois finally stopped smiling. "We raised $84.50."

Josh couldn't keep the news from changing his expression. *Not even $100. That's less than I could get panhandling.*

"We would do more if we could," Lois quickly answered. "Josh, we tried our best. Maybe people are just too diet-conscious this year."

Azzie came in with three more trays of cookies and set them down between Lois and Josh. "You guys should try these Rocky Road brownies. They're amazing."

Josh turned slightly towards him. "Azzie, we raised $84, and you're talking about sampling cookies? We'll all be volunteers at this rate."

Lois frowned, directing her matriarchal pre-wrath at Josh. "I'm disappointed, too, Josh. We put a lot of hours into this. Don't you think your volunteers wanted to do more?"

"Of course you do—and I am grateful—but if you had asked, I could have told you not to overestimate the power of a bake sale to meet the support needs of this ministry."

Azzie's eyes widened slightly as Lois turned the full force of her glare on Josh. "Um, I think I'm going to go make sure your trunk is closed, Lois," Azzie mumbled. "And, uh, yours too, Josh." He beat a hasty retreat out of the office.

Lois waited a moment before coldly responding to Josh. "'The support needs of this ministry?' The only support that was lacking this weekend was *your* support of *us*. We could do anything—we want to do anything—but the only thing you see when you look at us is harmless old grannies!"

Josh grimaced. *Ouch. This is hardly the textbook case of volunteer recognition.* "Lois, you're right. I'm genuinely sorry. You put a huge amount of effort into this bake sale. I know you're as disappointed as I am—maybe even more disappointed."

"Joshua Stiller, you missed my point."

Uh-oh. She used my full name. "Lois, I'm totally serious. I'm sorry. I'm a jerk. You and your friends did a bake sale yesterday while I took a nap after church. The least I could have done is to drop by and buy a tray of these cookies."

"Josh!" Lois fumed. "It's not about you being a jerk. And it's not about these cookies! It's about your view of *us*." She sighed, softening slightly. "You think that a bake sale is the best we can do. But there's so much more we want to do. And we can't get there because when it comes to donors your sole focus is 'the support needs of this ministry.' We're cogs in your fundraising wheel, Josh. And small cogs at that."

Josh lowered his head. He felt like one of the kids he counseled— hit hard with a truth, wanting to protest or run or get up and storm out, doubting that would do any good, and experiencing the sneaking sensation that someone who loved him very much was telling him something that he probably really needed to hear, even if he couldn't understand it yet.

"Lois . . ." Josh's voice trailed off as he slid to the floor, back against the wall, making himself as small and low as he felt inside. "What do you have in mind?"

If it were a bid for mercy, Lois wasn't buying. "What do I have in mind? What do I have in mind? I have in mind to help these kids get off drugs, and stay off the streets, and stay out of trouble, and all I'm doing is bake sales! I want to bring all of my friends down here and help transform the neighborhood, but the only thing I'm transforming is your waistline." She narrowed her gaze right on him. "I want to help kids, Josh. That's what I have in mind."

A minute passed, maybe more. Lois continued her laser focus on Josh, and Josh continued his effort to look pitiful. Finally he looked up at her.

"Lois, I didn't get into this ministry to spend so much of my time fundraising. I got into this ministry to *help kids*. I don't know what anyone else is called to do. That's between them and God. All I know is what God called me to do. And I know that every day that goes by I spend less time doing that and more time doing fundraising." He shook his head. "If I could just get somebody who all they did was work with donors, that would free me up so much and I really think more kids in this neighborhood could be helped. Why can't anyone else see that?"

"Maybe," said Lois, who Josh suspected hadn't blinked since she entered the building, "Maybe it's you that can't see something, Josh. *Maybe what you can't see is that these kids need more than you.*" Josh could hear the hum of traffic outside, the slight shudder of the building as a truck passed. His eyes wandered from file cabinet to Azzie's unoccupied desk to the tie that was still on the ground from last week. Anything to avoid Lois's gaze.

"These kids need me and a lot of other folks, too, Josh," Lois fairly well whispered. "Doing something more than baking cookies for you and folding your newsletters."

Sounds like "Prelude to a Resignation," mused Josh. He pictured Lois out in the street with a tray of cookies, offering scotchmellows to gang members in the midst of a drug deal. He pictured himself folding newsletters. *Azzie is such a coward. Or maybe he's been on her side all along.*

Lois stopped waiting for him to respond. "Josh, I've lived in this neighborhood for fifty years. I've seen my kids—and my grandkids—go through all the hell you try to keep kids out of. I've seen politicians and pastors and crusaders come and go. Each one was sure he could fix the problem. Each one had a plan, a ministry, city council money, supporters—everything. But sooner or later, each one concluded that the people weren't supportive enough, or the kids were not appreciative enough, or the hours in the day not long enough. But do you know what they overlooked?"

Josh raised his eyebrows, waiting for Lois's reply.

"That God favors peculiar armies."

Josh smiled, albeit reluctantly. He knew instantly that Lois was right, that God had chosen this morning and this woman to answer his question, *God, why aren't you blessing this?* He began to think through all the army stories in the Bible, from Gideon to David to the children of Israel and the crazy stories of how the Promised Land was won. He thought of the widow's mite story again, and in his mind's eye the widow was Lois. *Jesus, the multiplier of the mites.*

"Alright, Lois," he said, showing stirrings of life for the first time since he had slid to the floor under Lois's one-two verbal punch. "Peculiar armies. I think you're right. So," he nodded to the cookie ziggurat, "What do you intend to do with our peculiar ammunition?"

"Your work. I want to do it, too." She pointed to the cookies again. "How many kids in this neighborhood have never had a home-baked cookie in their lunch? Most of their moms are too drugged to make them one. How about I take all the cookies down to Frederick Douglass Elementary, or the Middle School, and hand them out?"

Josh nodded, slowly at first and then enthusiastically. "Lois, you may be on to something. Go for it." He sprang off the floor. "Dream and see what you can do. Take the cookies—better yet, take the entire bake sale team and their cookies—and go give a cookie to every kid at Frederick Douglass. You know, LLF works with teens, but it can't hurt to get some good PR going around the neighborhood."

This could be good, thought Josh. *She gets to give away cookies, I keep working with the teens, the bake sale committee is happy—a volunteer disaster narrowly averted.*

"Well, if I get to them first, maybe there will be less for you and Azzie to do when they become teens."

And get you involved in some way. We'll all end up happy if this works.

Lois grabbed four trays of cookies, stacking them precariously and holding them together with her chin. "Start moving cookies, Josh. I need to get them there by lunch. And find Azzie. Since he likes taste-tasting them so much, he can hand them out. I could use the help carrying them, anyway." She set her cookies down and pulled a behemoth cell-phone from her large purse. "Actually, I want to call Mary Ellen. She was afraid we would just throw out her scotchmellows, but since we aren't just tossing the cookies, maybe she'll want to hand some cookies out, too."

Josh began piling his cookie trays and moving them to the car. *This . . . this is amazing! What have I done? God, what have you done? This certainly wasn't me. I mean, the bake sale going south was lame. We really need the money, but this? I couldn't dream of this coming from a bake sale.*

Wait . . . Josh set the first batch of trays down and stood there. *What was that about a donor connection? Forget cookies. Where's Azzie?* He trotted back into the portable and burst into the office. "Azzie, I've got it!"

"You've got what?" Azzie stopped working on his lesson plan for the teen dads meeting. "Are there more things in heaven and earth, Horatio, than are dreamt of in your philosophy?"

"Dude, lay off the Shakespeare. I know what we're going to do with the cookies . . . and I think I just realized that our new philosophy does work!" Josh rifled through the piles on his desk and unburied the whiteboard with the *Question of the Moment.* "The connection between donors? I just saw it happen!"

"O day and night, but this is wondrous strange!"

"Azzie, now you're being ridiculous. Inner city kids that went to Bible college don't quote Shakespeare. You're making me feel dumb—will you let me share my moment of brilliance? I had an epiphany."

"An epiphany." Azzie read the whiteboard question. "'What if the connection between donors is as important, if not more important . . .'" he hesitated, "than the connection to the ministry?' How does this relate to cookies? No one bought any, so now I get to snack on them. As lame as no paycheck is, these cookies are good."

"That's why we're giving them to the kids."

"The kids?" Azzie looked at the collection of cookies and confections cluttering the office. "What kids? I don't have any, and yours probably shouldn't eat that many cookies."

"The kids at Douglass—Lois is bringing all the cookies to them."

"Huh." Azzie nodded sincerely. "Of course. That makes sense. Their teachers will love us." He shook his head. "Something tells me I'm missing something here."

"The connection to the donors!" *Okay, stop. You're missing something. Breathe. What haven't you told him?* "You heard my conversation with Lois, right?"

"The one where you said something dumb and then her eyes were like light sabers? Yeah, I heard part of it. She wants to do more than a bake sale."

"She said she wants *us* to support *her* doing the ministry. I was like, 'Um, are you kidding?' and she said that *she* didn't want to support *us*. She wants to do it—to do our job. She said she wants to do more if we'll let her."

"So she's giving away cookies from a failed bake sale?" Azzie asked skeptically.

"No—I mean, yes—well, sort of. She pointed out that most kids at Douglass come from homes that are too broken to have real, homemade cookies in their lunches—if they even get a homemade lunch—and we have a bunch of cookies, so let's give them cookies."

"Okay. That makes sense. So how does the donor connection fit in?"

"Well, I'm helping her carry cookies, and she starts calling the bake sale committee to come hand out cookies with her over lunch. They're all retired, so they can do that. They all like kids, so that works. They all like cookies, so they can feel like they're using their work. And they're all excited! Like, more excited than I am."

Azzie shook his head. "That would be impressive."

"Dude, it's awesome! I'm . . . I'm still geeking out over it! It's like—"

"Josh, choose your language carefully," said Azzie, raising an index finger sagely. "Twain said the difference between the almost right word and the right word was the difference between lightning and a lightning bug. You gotta make sure you get it right."

"Shakespeare is geeky. Geeky is the right word."

"Says the man who just said he's geeking out. Twentysomethings can like Shakespeare and still be cool. Maybe even double-cool for understanding the Bard."

Josh sighed. "Anyway, Lois wants you to help her move cookies, and go to the school with her over lunch." Josh pulled out the large white board, trying to find empty space between the amoebas of network connections. "We need a new white board." He went into the reception area and pulled the extra white board from the teaching area. "The donor—Lois—just got involved directly in our ministry, or in the cause. She is doing the ministry and I support her to be successful. She is using her skills to spread our shared cause in her sphere of influence—the bake sale committee. And we're supporting her in that."

"So as a ministry . . . are we supposed to be *doing* the ministry or *supporting* people doing the ministry?"

"I guess . . ." Josh rubbed his chin. "I guess both. Maybe that's what we do with donors. They give money, and then we let them do the ministry." Josh wrote that on the white board. "That works, doesn't it?"

Azzie took the pen and reversed the statement. "What if . . . what if *they* do the ministry, and then they want *us* to give them money?"

"What did Lois do?" Josh pointed at Azzie with the marker. "She gave, and now she's getting involved."

Azzie interrupted. "Are you sure that was first? She was involved, but not through us. She's lived in this neighborhood for how long? She didn't just one day up and decide to give. I think she was involved in her own ways, and just saw us as a way to help with that."

"So . . ." Azzie tapped his lips with his fingertips. "So we get people involved and then they become donors? I guess that would work. Our ministry is to work with teens . . . and to get other people to work with teens? Can we do both?"

Azzie wrote *fundraising* above Josh's scrawlings on donor involvement. "If, instead of doing major donor calls that don't work, we did this? Yeah. I think so."

"But what about the major donors?" asked Josh. "They aren't down here doing the ministry. How will we ever get major gifts if we only focus on getting the Loises of the world involved?" Josh took the pen and drew a line between *fundraising* and his white board musings. "We'll have to do both."

"Man, maybe there is no 'both.'" Azzie smudged the line with his thumb. "What if our major donor calls became cookie calls? Like, instead of going to the fancy restaurant and talking golf, we challenge them to come down here and hand out cookies with

> *Fundraising*
>
> They give the money, and then we let them do the ministry.
>
> What if *they* do the ministry, and then they want *us* to give them money?

Lois. Let them do what we're doing. Let them see the kids, see the neighborhood, and touch the projects—like Lois does."

"So . . ." Josh stepped back to survey the board in total. "You're saying our fundraising becomes training the donors to do our work? Do you really think they'll still give?"

"Do you think Lois will stop giving because we train her to do the ministry?"

"No." Josh tapped the board. "She already said she wouldn't—she wants to work with us. She's working through us. She always says that LLF has to stay in existence."

"Then maybe this is fundraising for us, man," said Azzie, looking up as Lois walked in. "I don't know how other ministries do it, but this sure beats what we're doing now. Lois doesn't even look like she's gonna kill you anymore."

Lois smiled with an exaggerated nose wrinkle. "Just his waistline. Azzie, can you help me take these cookies over to Douglass?"

Azzie stood up and grabbed his keys. "One cookie delivery guy coming . . . as long as I get one more of those Rocky Road Brownies. And the recipe. If I ever find a girlfriend, I'm going to make these for her."

"Deal. I'll even teach you how to make them." She handed him the last tray of brownies. "But you better hope your lady-friend likes chocolate."

"She'll *have* to like chocolate, man. How could anyone not like chocolate? And how could I ever apologize to her if she doesn't like chocolate?" Azzie grabbed his keys from a small bird feeder on his desk.

"Maybe I'll woo her with Shakespeare. Do you think Shakespeare is cool, Lois?"

"Shakespeare? Oh, I guess, if you like strange-sounding words. I never had much use for him in my life."

"Use? Lois, how can you pragmatically turn Shakespeare into . . ." Josh shut his office door as they left, drowning out the sounds of Azzie supporting his favorite bard. *That kid will learn some day. Until he does, he can convert as many people as he wants to his Shakespeare obsession.*

He slapped his head.

How could I miss that? Azzie is a Shakespeare-cause-spreader! He's trying to spread Shakespeare to his entire sphere of influence, one quote at a time.

But it's not like he's trying to get people to give him money—he's just excited about Shakespeare, and that makes him spread his cause.

Are donors really like that? Lois is, but she's special. This is her ministry, and so she wants to spread it. Not all donors think of this as their ministry. We're just another ministry. Why would they spread anything we do? We're nothing special to them.

We are special to Lois . . . And all these people did care enough to bake cookies . . . Maybe we're more special to them than I think? Or maybe the cause is the real draw, and we're hiding it under a bushel.

We need to raise up that cause. Lois is right—these kids need a lot more than me. If they want to spread cookies, they can spread cookies. Lois and her baking team are the ones doing the work. They're the ones spreading this cause today. It isn't me. The donors themselves are doing this without me, and what they are doing is pretty cool. Donors can do more of this ministry if I let them. Maybe donors even need to do this . . . which, I guess, makes my job one of spreading my cause to them so that they can spread it to others. I need to make them excited about spreading it. They can spread it way faster than I did, because they didn't get the idea stuck in their head that somehow they were God's gift to this cause.

Josh pulled out his newest white board and removed the line between *fundraising* and his scribblings about donors.

This would be fundraising? How crazy is this? I'm spreading the ministry to donors—as I still continue to do it—and then they fundraise? Just because they're excited? There's no way this can work . . . but it sounds cool. Azzie's right. We might as well try it.

He took the *Question of the Moment* white board and added the numeral two. *What if the donor is the one spreading the ministry within his or her network?* Josh thought for a moment and erased that. *What if the donor is the primary way of spreading the ministry*—he erased ministry—*the shared cause within his or her network?*

Spreading the shared cause, Josh thought. *This could get interesting.*

QUESTION OF THE MOMENT

1. What if the relationship between donors is as important as the relationship between the donor and our ministry?

2. What if the donor is the primary way of spreading the shared cause within his or her network?

To Ponder

1. Set your ministry cause aside for a moment. What "hobby-causes" do you have that you spread like Azzie spreads Shake-speare? Why do you do it? How do you do it? How do people respond to you?

2. What is the difference between spreading the cause and spread-ing your organization? In your ministry, who has the responsi-bility for spreading your cause? Who are your best advocates? What have you done to support them? How much of the minis-try you do are they capable of doing? Does your estimate match what Scripture says?

3. Do you have examples in your ministry where the relationship between donors became as important as their relationship to your organization? How did those instances come about? What was your role in facilitating?

4. Have you provided the tools and opportunities your donors need to spread your shared cause? Have you provided them opportunities to actively *do* your ministry instead of just support your work?

5. If you were going to switch your fundraising program from raising money for your organization to training others to raise money for the cause, what one step could you take before lunchtime today? Why not try it before you turn the page?

Chapter 3

"**J**osh, I can't do this. Things have been getting worse. Shiana can't handle her . . . our kid. Her parents are back on drugs and she wants to move in with my g'ma. She said something about her dad knocking her around again."

Josh had assumed Azzie's place at the head of a circle-ish configuration of chairs and was finishing up a meeting with the teen dads support group. Five of the guys from the meeting had already left—one to work at the nearest Burger King, the rest to finish up homework.

After two hours, Josh was done sitting properly in a chair. Like the hip youth worker he was, he turned the chair around backward and wrapped his legs around the back of it, facing the remaining teen in the office. Derek, the only non-senior and the newest addition to the group, was sitting contemplatively across from him.

Josh nodded slowly. *God, these two really need you. How they and little Naomi will make it through in one piece is beyond me.* "Derek, what does it mean if she moves in with your grandma?"

Derek grinned slightly. "I'm not sleeping with her, if that's what you're asking. I've learned. I'll be out on the couch again, and she and Naomi can have my room."

"What does your grandma think?"

He snorted. "She's probably too drunk to notice a few extra people, and Shiana's already around a lot. Most of the time, my grandma is asleep before Shiana leaves. Even if she did notice, she won't care. It's not like she's around enough to be a real g'ma."

So he wants a real grandma. I wonder if Lois wants a few more grandkids, or even great grandkids. If the volunteers want to do more to help kids, I wonder how I can connect them to kids like Derek? It's not like I can just send donors over to Derek's house, and these kids need more than cookies. But, they don't need substance abuse recovery, or anything like that. They just need some stable adults in their lives.

Derek leaned back in his metal chair and crossed his arms. "My brother was telling me something about cookies happening at Douglass. He thought that was pretty cool. He was all like, 'Yeah! Scotch— something or other.'"

"Scotchmellow. Cookies. Not alcohol." Josh smiled. "Lois and some of her friends made a bunch of cookies for a bake sale to try to raise money for us, but they didn't sell. She decided to take them down to the elementary school."

"He said he saw Azzie there, which made me realize you probably had something to do with it." Derek struck up a pretend-pout pose. "Punk didn't save me a cookie."

Josh smiled, then got serious. "Derek, let me ask you something. If I could get you a grandma like Lois who made you cookies, would you take it? A sort of mentorship thing for you and Shiana?"

"Mentor? Aren't you already doing that?"

"Yeah, and we would keep doing that. It would be an extra . . . a real grandma for you. She could make you cookies, and teach you and Shiana how to cook, or show you what to do when Naomi is being fussy, or anything."

"So . . . like foster care except for big kids?"

"Not foster care. I mean more like . . . like my job, except doing things only grandmas can do." He leaned back in his chair. "We all need grandmas, right?"

Derek shrugged. "Sure, man. That's cool. Whatever. I'd be down with that." He stood up and returned his chair to the wall of the room.

"Hey Josh," he said, stopping and spinning around. "Naomi has her six-month birthday this Friday. Do you think we could do something like at lunch? Start that grandma thing up now, you know?"

"Friday?" Josh checked his Blackberry. Blocked out. *My Bob Kemmis meeting. I've been working so hard with him . . . he's so close to giving. He could be the major donor that puts me in the black.* "I'm booked solid, Derek . . . ."

Derek's shoulders dropped. "Oh. Okay. That's cool." He frowned, hesitating to go.

A donor meeting? A donor meeting can't be more important than this kid's life. He and his girlfriend already made the tough choice. They kept the kid. And Derek—he looks up to me like a dad. I'm not going to be that dad that has too many business meetings for my kids.

"Actually, Derek," blurted Josh. "Tell you what. I have a meeting, but I can end it early. Or have Azzie cover. Or something. Bring Naomi and Shiana. And the other guys from the group."

Derek nodded. "Yeah. Okay. That'd be cool. I'm cool with that." He put on his black coat and white hat. "See you later, Joshy Baby. Thanks for today."

Josh relaxed and sighed as Derek left. *What am I going to do with Bob Kemmis? I'm throwing a birthday party for a six-month-old—with a bunch of unmarried teen parents—at the same time I'm supposed to be meeting a guy who actually could end up being our first major donor? What am I supposed to do with that? Azzie's good, but he can't cover the major donor meeting. And Derek asked me to be there. I have to be there for the kid. He needs some consistent, positive male interaction.*

I could get Bob to help with the party. No. Absolutely not. These kids are not ready for major donor prime time. Maybe I should just see . . .

Azzie and Lois entered, interrupting his train of thought. Both were holding trays of cookies, and Lois was positively spritely for someone her age. "Josh, you should have seen the kids—they were so excited. They kept calling me 'G-ma Lois'!"

Josh smiled broadly. "That's great! I think you found your niche." He frowned. "But why are there leftover cookies? Did half the kids skip today?"

Azzie shook his head. "I'm fairly certain we had more kids this week than last week."

"Then how on earth do you have extra cookies?"

Azzie shrugged and pointed to Lois. "Not my fault. I did the best I could."

Lois nodded. "He was a firm believer in handing out a cookie, trying a cookie, handing out another cookie, and trying another cookie."

"Why then the world's mine oyster," Azzie retorted, "which I with cookie will open."

Josh rolled his eyes. "Come on, guys. We had ten dozen last time and it was barely enough."

Lois shrugged innocently. "I just made a few phone calls . . . talked to a few ladies at church yesterday. They were all very excited, so I didn't want to leave anyone out."

Azzie nodded. "We had 20 women show up at lunch today . . . and they each brought at least one dozen cookies. At least. We gave a bunch to all the students, all the teachers, all the staff, left some in the staff lounge, and still had a few dozen to give to the newscasters."

Josh's eyes widened. "Newscasters?"

"Newscasters," Lois repeated proudly. "The son of one of the ladies I told works for Channel 8. He thought the idea was brilliant, so he got the news down there. He said we wouldn't make the evening news tonight, but they might use it as a feature sometime."

Azzie shrugged again. "So basically they filmed us handing out cookies, interviewed some of the kids, talked to me and Lois, asked one or two other ladies why they were there, talked to the teachers—it was cool! You should have been there."

We work to reach druggies in the streets and can't seem to stir any support, and the minute we share a few cookies the world is knocking at our door. We have volunteers come out of the woodwork, and even TV stations. Oh, irony.

"I can't believe you got all those extra cookies from all those people," Josh said.

"It was dope, man," Azzie said, plunging into his desk chair. "I mean, it was cookies, but it was dope—you know, cool. The ladies were all like sharing with the kids, and they were all like way more excited than at a bake sale where nobody's buying and everybody's all suspicious of you trying to interrupt their shopping and stuff. They were in the zone, man—handing out cookies, hugging little kids, making new friends. It was dope."

The zone? The cookie zone? Cookie ministry isn't exactly our vision. If it will give us a door into these kids' lives before they get into trouble, that's great. But a cookie zone?

Lois nodded enthusiastically to Azzie's commentary. "We got to do what we grandmas do best, and they want to do it again. They said to call them whenever we need help—they'll do anything, and they really want to do more."

"More? Funny you should mention that, Lois . . . ," mused Josh, remembering the train of thought he had left idling when Azzie and Lois had entered. "Just today we had a teen asking why he doesn't get grandmas bringing cookies to the high school."

Lois nodded excitedly. "We could start a cookie branch for the middle school, and a cookie branch for the high school. Cookies everywhere!" She grabbed a box of leftover cookies from the chair. "I'll take these home with me and hand them out to people who want to help. That will be fun."

"Speaking of fun," Josh added, "Do you want to decorate for a birthday party? Derek and Shiana's daughter is going to be six months old this Friday, and Azzie and I aren't very good at the artistic side of stuff."

"It's true. Look at this office." Lois shook her head. "I'll be here Friday. Derek and Shiana's little girl deserves a proper birthday party." Her eyes twinkled a little. "I haven't done a birthday party in years. This will be so much fun." She carried her box out to her car and left.

Azzie shook his head. "The lady is going to turn our entire ministry upside down. What's next? Cookie sponsorships?"

"You know, Azzie, that's actually not a half-baked idea. Sponsor a cookie for a kid. We're going to need to replace that bake sale money somehow."

"Yeah—$84 doesn't exactly grow on trees." Azzie walked back into the office and pulled out the whiteboard, erasing their previous notes on supporting donors. "So I think this cookie thing just turned into something way bigger than we were thinking. So do we do something to try to make this last, or . . . ?"

"I think you already nailed it, Azzie—sponsor a cookie. That will give folks a way to donate to us, and then Lois can grow this cookie ministry as big as she's able to sponsor." Josh took the pen and wrote *Cookie Sponsorship.* "This could be interesting—way more potential for funds than the bake sale, and it's actually helping kids. Brilliant."

"Brilliant works for me." Azzie rested his head back on his chair. "Handing out cookies was tiring, man."

"I bet kids getting cookies are more receptive to talking than junior and senior guys in a dads support group." Josh schlumped into his own chair. "I got to talk with Derek a little more today, and it left me cornered. He wants to have a six-month-old party for Naomi this Friday, but originally I had a meeting scheduled with Bob Kemmis."

"So Derek the dad beat out the big time maybe-donor? That works with the ministry but sure doesn't raise any money."

Azzie sat up a bit. "What if we invite Kemmis to the party? Let him see what we do. That's better than just talking about it all the time."

"I thought about it, but . . . a donor? At a birthday party for a six-month-old? With the Not Ready For Prime Time Players in our dads group? I can mess up our chances with Bob well enough on my own, thank you very much."

Azzie tapped his desk. "Beats cancelling on him, dude. You know—give him a walking tour of the neighborhood . . . hope we don't get held up . . . though recruiting teens to hold up donors could be a good fundraiser for us."

"Albeit slightly unethical."

Josh returned to the white board. "Cookie sponsorship, huh? Major donor prospects eating birthday cake at birthday parties for six-month-old children of unmarried teenagers. This is the stuff they don't teach you in books."

Azzie grinned. "Lois said she was all done doing bake sales, and that she's gonna outnumber teen gangs with an LLF Cookie Gang."

Josh looked at the board and frowned. "But all cookies and cake and no dinner. How nutritious can that be for our budget?"

"Nah—cookies are just the start, man." Azzie stepped to the board and redrew the spaghetti network for Josh, showing donors connecting to donors around the ministry. "Look what Lois is doing. She's telling all her friends—getting her whole church in on the thing—because she's all involved and excited. She's probably told forty people about us and the cookie ministry." Azzie was drawing more and more spaghetti. "If she gets those forty people to each go tell two friends . . ."

". . . Then that's a lot of cookies—right. But if they don't give, we're still stuck in the red." Josh returned dejectedly to his desk chair. "Giving isn't the end goal, Azzie. It's ministry. We both know that. But even if we corner the market on cookie donors, if we can't get people to move beyond cookies, then the rest of the ministry isn't going to happen. We at least need some sort of overhead off the top to finance the ministry that's supposed to be supporting these people. If the ministry doesn't exist, we can't support the people who want to be involved."

Azzie nodded, a bit reluctantly.

"Maybe we just have to keep doing donor work on the side, Azzie. I don't know. Lois can keep doing her cookie deal, and we can keep doing what we've been doing—meet with teens and then spend most of our time begging donors for money."

Both of them sat silently, attempting to return to Monday mundaneness after the sobering dialogue.

Josh spent more time shuffling papers on his desk than actually trying to reorganize what appeared to be an explosion of paper.

Maybe we were off on the whole thing, thought Josh. *Maybe the donor-connected-to-donor network thing is just a cool idea that is really just unrelated to major donor fundraising. It was the Question of the Moment, but that moment didn't last very long. I think it lasted right up until we came into contact with reality.*

Reality isn't very nice to major donor fundraising. Then again . . .

Azzie's right. Inviting Bob Kemmis on Friday can't diminish our chances any lower than they are right now.

With time, the Monday mundaneness and depressing discourse faded into the distance. Friday came quickly, bringing a baby birthday party—and a donor meeting—in the same place, at the same time. Lois arrived early Friday afternoon with a cohort of retired women from her church, each bringing decorations, baby birthday presents, basic necessities for any young couple and, of course, years of advice for Derek and Shiana.

Josh chuckled as he watched two ladies, both with canes and osteoporosis, try to coach Azzie on the proper placement of multi-colored streamers for the best aesthetic results. *That poor kid. He's acting like he's color-blind . . . or just blind. I don't remember ever adding PR person to the retirement community in his job description . . . but he's good at it.*

Josh meandered out into the reception area, trying to appear relaxed in his overly-dressy rumpled polo shirt and khakis. *Bob is running late . . . I was really hoping we could get a chance to talk and explain all this before Derek and company showed up.* Josh looked up in anticipation as the door opened, but it was a few birthday party guests. The ladies immediately recruited them into tying balloons around the room, not wasting any available help.

Josh finally gave up watching the door and retreated into his office. *I suppose in a way it would be nice if Bob skipped . . . I could devote all of my attention to Derek, which he would appreciate, and Azzie and I wouldn't have to juggle a sales pitch to a rich guy and a birthday party for an impoverished family.*

Azzie knocked on the door. "Bob just walked in. Want me to send him in or want to come out?"

Josh jumped up quickly and tucked in his shirt. "I'll come out. Did you explain all the commotion?"

"Nope. He asked if we throw a party every time we convince somebody to stop by our office."

Josh winced. "I think Bob Kemmis thinks there are four members to the Trinity. Whether he's the original or an honorary member . . ." Josh shrugged. "I'll go see him. Is Derek here yet?"

"Not yet. He called to say he was running late."

Josh ducked under the crepe streamers in front of his door and shook Bob's hand. "Bob, how does today find you?"

Bob was a sixty-something, semi-retired lawyer. Years of arguing cases and compiling volumes of exhibits had left him cynical, gruff, and very nearsighted. If the world didn't already revolve around him, he could find some way to change the orbit.

He grunted. "It's Friday. I'm ready to be home . . . though my wife is babysitting all the grandkids tonight, so I won't get any peace there." Bob gestured with his head to the streamers around the room. "Who's the party for?"

"One of the teens I mentor," Josh answered, trying to sound as casual as if he hosted donor/neighborhood birthday party combos every day. "He's in our teen dad support group, and his daughter is turning six months today. It's a pretty big milestone, considering that a year ago, he was pushing his girlfriend to have an abortion. We're helping him and his girlfriend celebrate."

"Girlfriend?" Bob looked around the room at the couples of teens, each with their own young child in tow. "These kids aren't married?"

Josh shook his head, trying to encourage Bob into the back room of the office before he said something really stupid . . . really loudly. "All of these kids are still finishing high school, but all plan on getting married as soon as they graduate. They're really doing their best to keep their lives on the right path." He opened the door to the back office. *Bob, you're killing me. These kids are having a birthday party. Let's go someplace quiet where we can talk.*

Bob wasn't going into the office. "A birthday party? You're doing one of these for a couple of teenagers?"

"Sure. We're . . . we're pretty much the only stable adult figures in these kids' lives. Their parents are either gone or so drugged that they aren't there for these kids."

"What about grandparents? If they have parents, they have to have grandparents," Bob suggested. "How come their grandparents aren't doing this?"

"If their grandparents are around, they're in the same mess as their parents. Most of them don't have stable grandparents, either—half of them are living with their grandparents already, and their grandparents are typically in some form of substance abuse addiction, too."

Bob grunted again. "So you step in and take over?"

"Something like that. Azzie and I mentor a lot of the guys, and then Lois," Josh pointed to her. "She's been helping with all sorts of stuff. Last week she started a program to distribute home-made cookies to the kids over at Douglass Elementary."

"Say no to drugs and yes to cookies, huh?"

"Well, the cookies aren't really the point, Bob. These kids could get cookies from the store, or the cafeteria, or wherever. What they don't have is a grandma, or a mom, or someone who will make them a cookie and—and basically tell the kid that you care about him or her. They don't get the personalized attention that we take for granted when they come from broken homes. Most of the kids at Douglass are from broken homes, so Lois recruited several other ladies from the church to make cookies and bring them to all the kids. It's almost like they adopted the entire elementary school. If she could, she would be a grandmother to all of them."

Bob looked around at the balloons and streamers again. "A birthday party for a probably-would-have-been aborted child born to some teens still in high school and not yet married because they have no other adults in their broken lives to give them a real party or direction."

Uh-oh. Here it comes. Bob, please don't say anything in front of these kids. I need you and I need them. Don't alienate them. "We think it's a very tangible way to show them the love of Jesus Christ."

He grunted. "I like it, Josh. Who's the lucky dad of today's kid?"

Josh blinked, surprised by Bob's approval. "Uh . . . Derek is. He and he and his girlfriend aren't quite here yet. Azzie said they were running late."

"Perfect." Bob walked out of the office.

Josh stared after him, stunned. He shrugged in response to Azzie's quizzical look.

Bob came back in the door a few moments later, carrying a small, gift-wrapped box. "I told you my wife is babysitting the grandkids. I picked up a few goodies for the youngest on the way home from work today, but . . . well, I think Derek and his girlfriend, and their kid, could use it more than my spoiled grandkids."

"Bob . . . wow. I actually thought you might have been leaving. I don't know what to say." *Do I offer a receipt, or . . . ?*

"Say thanks, Josh, and let's get on with this party. Is there cake?"

"Uh, cake—yes. And presents. This is a real birthday party for some very real kids with some very real needs."

Bob grunted again. "Yes. Needs. Lots of needs. I figured that you would be another one of those guys who tells me all about his needs, or the ministry needs—how you guys are struggling to make ends meet and how you need my money to make it happen. If that had happened, I probably would have walked out—I'm old and don't have time for that. I've heard enough plea bargains in my life. But this—this, Josh, is impressive. You're the first to actually show me the needs of these kids, instead of your own needs."

"Well, thanks, Bob."

The first? We didn't even try! It's not like I meant to do that. I was planning on a nice, sterile meeting over my desk, with the teens and babies making a nice backdrop. Now the sterile meeting is the backdrop, and Bob wants to party?

Bob stayed through the rest of the party, leading an enthusiastically off-pitch round of happy birthday for Naomi and grousing on about the challenges of fatherhood with a group of teen dads over cake. A few hours later, the carnage of cake and crepe streamers was finally over. Most of the teens left to feed their hungry, sugar-buzzed children, and Bob remained behind to help Josh and Lois clean up the Friday afternoon damage.

Bob's still here . . . it's like he's waiting for me to ask him to give. He can't mean that . . . but I'd love to ask him for money. How do I ask him for money? How do I bring this up when he's busy cleaning up cake?

Bob brought a platter of cake over to the trash can next to Josh. "Nice party, Josh. I like it."

"Thanks. I think Derek and Shiana really appreciated your gifts and advice." He relieved Bob of the tray of cake and threw it away. "Is this something that you'd like to help with in the future?"

"Why? Do you have more birthday parties planned? Or do you want me to help hand out cookies?" Bob stared at him, almost daring him to respond. "We were going to meet about me giving. Is that what you want?"

"I'm not going to deny that I'd like you to stay involved with this. You've seen what we do. Is this something that you want to keep helping with, in some way or another?"

"Sure. I can pray for you guys."

Bob stared at Josh with a deadpan expression for about ten seconds before chuckling and squeezing Josh's shoulder with a Vulcan death pinch.

"Josh, your expression is priceless. Yes, I want to be involved. I wrote a check to you this morning, and I've had it in my back pocket all day today. I had no intention of sticking around to meet with you— I decided to give you this check long before today."

"Then . . . then why did you come?" Josh stuttered. "You have so much to do. Why did you stay all day?"

"Because I care about this neighborhood. I occasionally like kids, occasionally even want to help them, and I was really hoping that I would get to see what you guys do here. Meeting in my office doesn't do too much to help with that, so I thought I would come here and see what you did. If I was convinced, you'd get the check. If I didn't like it, I'd leave with my check."

Bob pointed to the sagging streamers. "I saw what you did. I like it." He pulled a check out of his back pocket. "Here, Josh. Call me the next time you have a birthday party or something. I want to stay involved. Use this to help Derek and his friends." Bob paused. "Actually, call me Monday morning. I'd like to stay involved, and I want to get some of my friends in on this. Come down to the office, and I'll introduce you to a few who might want to help." He turned on his heel and left.

Azzie huddled with Josh as soon as Bob left. "What just happened?"

"I'm not sure. He said that he didn't come here to give . . . just to see what we do and to get involved . . . and that he was already going to give. I didn't even really ask him for money. I asked if he wanted to stay involved."

"And . . . ?"

"And he made some sort of joke! It . . . it was so unlike him. I didn't even know the man could make a joke, but he did, and then he handed me a check, and then he left." Josh held out the check to Azzie. "I haven't looked. I'm kind of scared to look."

Azzie opened it, didn't say anything, and handed it back to Josh.

Josh couldn't resist the suspense any longer. He opened the check.

"Oh!"

The biggest gift we've ever gotten.

"$2,000? He gave us $2,000?"

Azzie nodded. "That's the biggest gift we've ever gotten! And all the guy did was come to a birthday party." He pulled a dangling streamer from the ceiling and tossed it into the trash. "We need to have more of these birthday parties."

"Bob said to come to his office . . ." mumbled a still-dazed Josh. "He said he would introduce me to some people he thinks should get involved. Maybe he means they'll want to give, too."

Josh took the check back into the office and locked it in the safe. "Remind me to go to the bank on Monday."

"As if you'll forget." Azzie sat down at his own desk.

"Bob just gave us $2,000. Why?" Josh pursed his lips against a finger pyramid, concentrating deeply. "It's not like we told him about our need. I don't even know what he wants us to spend the money on. 'Help Derek and Shiana'—that's what he said. He said it was because he was involved—just like Lois. And he wants to stay involved. And get his friends involved." He rubbed his face. "This whole involvement thing is really throwing me for a loop. I thought rich people gave money so they didn't have to get involved. Now our whole budget for the week just happened through involvement. What on earth do we do with that?"

"Fall on our knees and thank the God in heaven?"

"Well, yeah, but besides that? If the involved people are the ones giving, and the people who aren't involved aren't giving, well . . . that has to affect our fundraising, right?"

"Affect whether our paychecks bounce, yeah. Let me cash mine first this time, okay?"

"No, I'm serious." Josh strode over to the whiteboard. "Up until today, we asked some people for money, and then, if they didn't have any money, we let them get involved. What if we changed that? What if we focused on getting everyone involved, and then asked them to give?"

Azzie shrugged. "Makes sense, yeah. If they're involved, they see what we do. They start to want to give instead of wanting to leave the room when we start begging and all . . ."

Josh paused a moment. "So we need to let potential donors see the need for them and then equip them to meet the need themselves." Josh began scrawling on the whiteboard. "A random person gets involved . . . said random person becomes part of the solution. Said random person then decides to give."

"So fundraising happens as a result of giving people our problems to deal with? Now that's fundraising I could learn to love," said Azzie, crossing his arms and nodding approvingly.

"Yeah—strangely enough," muttered Josh. "We have the cause of helping teens. They have the cause of helping teens. We become the, uh, vessel by which they help teens. After they're involved, they decide to give to said vessel, to keep it, uh, vesseling."

"Vesseling?" Azariah raised his eyebrows. "Is that a word?"

"I just made it up," Josh announced triumphantly. "Shakespeare got to make up words."

"You're not Shakespeare, dude."

"Well, the dictionary isn't closed," said Josh with finality. "These people give to the vessel to keep it vesseling."

"Or if you were speaking English, you'd say that they give to keep us helping them help teens."

Josh shook his head slowly, tapping the board with the marker. "Man, that's a paradigm shift. Who came up with this crazy idea?" He took out the *Question of the Moment* board. "I guess we did."

"We did, and now we get to vessel it," Azzie said, surveying the board with his hands on his hips.

"Well, try *this*, fellow vessel," mumbled Josh, writing out the following on the board. *What if fundraising is a result of helping*—he wiped out the last word with his thumb—*equipping ordinary people to solve the problems we solve and share the cause we love?*

"So the focus changes from fundraising as a process to fundraising as a result of a process?" Azzie nodded. "I like it. I think we just had greatness thrust upon us."

"Greatness . . . or too much cake. We'll see how this goes." Josh capped the pen and hung his *Question of the Moment* white board on his desk. "Let it be written, let it . . . try to be done."

QUESTION OF THE MOMENT

1. What if the relationship between donors is as important as the relationship between the donor and our ministry?

2. What if the donor is the primary way of spreading the shared cause within his or her network?

3. What if . . . fundraising is a result of equipping ordinary people to solve the problems we solve and share the cause we love?

To Ponder

1. Have you attempted to insulate donors from the actual problems your ministry is working to solve while immersing them in your organization's financial needs? What would happen if you reversed that—insulating your donors from your organization's financial needs while immersing them in the actual problems your ministry is trying to solve?

2. What are three things you do in ministry that you think a donor or volunteer could never get involved in? Ask yourself why? How would Lois respond to you? What about Bob?

3. What is the difference between a donor and a volunteer? Are you sure it is a valid and helpful distinction? Are "donor" and "volunteer" scriptural concepts? Why or why not? What words does Scripture use to describe people like Lois and Bob?

4. If you were Josh, what would be your next step in interacting with Lois and her friends? How about Bob and his friends? Are there any other donor "networks" in the story that Josh has not recognized yet? If so, which ones? What would be your next step with these?

5. List five places or moments in your ministry that may be good venues for a donor meeting. What donor or prospective donor can you invite to each one in the near future?

Chapter 4

$\mathbf{J}$osh was beaming as Azzie came into the office the following Monday morning.

"You'll never guess who just called me," he challenged. Azzie sat down at his desk and tossed his back pack under his chair. "Um, Lois. She has more cookie bakers?"

"Even better," Josh said, rubbing his hands together. "Bob Kemmis."

"It's been . . ." Azzie checked his watch, ". . . less than three days since he left, and he's already calling? I thought you were supposed to call him."

"I was going to call him, but I didn't want to appear too eager. So imagine my surprise when *he* called *me* just a few minutes ago! He said that he and his wife were having their church fellowship group over to their house tonight for dessert, so I might as well come over and talk about LLF."

"Tonight?" Azzie's eyes widened "First he drops a big check on us, and then *he* calls *you* a few days later and invites *you* to *his* house for dinner?" Azzie shook his head and let out a long and satisfied sigh. "Your days of begging are over, man."

"Don't count your cookies yet, young charge," mumbled Josh as he stood up from his desk and began rummaging through past newsletters and brochures. "I still have to go and take the order, and I have less than twelve hours to prepare. So what do you think would be good to take to this fellowship group? Bunch of Westsiders . . . probably never been down on our side of town before."

He stopped suddenly after closing a file cabinet drawer.

"Azzie," he said solemnly. "This meeting tonight could fund our whole ministry for the year. I mean, given how fired up Bob was when he left here—if he moves in a circle of people like himself—I could feasibly be walking back in here tomorrow with a *stack* of checks like the one Bob gave us last week." He frowned and looked at Azariah. "That's slightly intimidating, you know?"

"It's a dream come true, man" Azzie corrected. "How many ministries would want to be in our shoes today? This is our big break, J—we have a major donor who actually gave us something and then called *you* and said, 'Hey, come meet all my friends.'" Azariah flipped on his computer, watching it whirr and click its way slowly back to life. "Goodbye bake sales. Hello pipeline from the Westside!"

"We're not doing bake sales again, anyways," Josh retorted. "No matter what happens tonight, Lois has transformed into the Cookie Monster. She'll never sell another cookie again, that's for sure."

He returned to his desk and checked his calendar. "Teen dads are in today, Az. You're on it?"

"Unless I get a call to head to the Westside, yeah."

Josh smiled. It was good to finally start the week relaxed and hopeful.

Still, I'd much rather be here with all the teens than over at Bob's house asking people for money, thought Josh. *But one night of asking could nail this budget for months. Finally I'd have some time freed up for real ministry.*

Josh grabbed a yellow steno pad from the top of the stack brimming full in his right desk drawer. *Finally, time to think and prepare like a normal ministry.* "Alright. Time to craft the ultimate in Westside presentations. Where do I begin to tell the story of an underfunded but highly loveable ministry?"

"How about a picture of me at the bank holding a paycheck that just bounced?" offered Azariah.

"No, I'm serious, Azzie." Josh rubbed his chin, cupping his face and squinting in concentration. "This needs to be polished . . . smooth . . . professional. People don't invest real dollars if they think you're a fly-by-night deal operating out of the back of a flatbed pickup truck. I want them to know that we're capable of handling their money and making a real difference with it."

He began to jot down bullet points. "Let's see. We know how to work with kids. We have a low overhead. Bob saw firsthand the difference we make every day. Wait . . ."

He returned to the closet and grabbed a stack of brochures.

"This ought to help. We did a pretty good job with this brochure."

"Except it's kinda old, J . . ." Azzie walked over and picked up one to review. "That was a lot of hair ago, man. You know, we should have taken some pictures of that birthday party Bob was at. And the cookie giveaway, too." Azzie set the brochure down. "You gonna tell them about the cookie sponsorship idea? Maybe see if they want to come and help us deliver?"

"Cookie sponsorships?" Josh grimaced. "C'mon Azzie—these are *rich* people. I'm trying to walk out of there tonight with our budget funded, not some tip to pay for sugar and flour and bacon grease, or whatever you put in cookies." He put his hands on Azzie's shoulders and was once again the younger man's counselor. "Azzie, the cookie project is great. It is. But this may be our one chance, man. Kemmis' fellowship group. They can do more than sponsor a cookie." He patted Azariah's shoulder and returned to his own desk. "I just need to know how to ask."

"Well, how did you ask with Bob?" Azariah sat on Josh's desk corner.

"I dunno . . ." He paused, leaning back in his chair as he tried to jog his memory. "I think I just asked him if he could come by the office instead of meeting me at the restaurant, so I could show him what we do." He flipped through the brochure again, looking for a muse. "I doubt he'd be too excited if I called him and told him to do that tonight."

"Well, maybe we should have another birthday party this Friday," Azzie half-joked. "Or a baby shower. We know any teens having babies?

"Several," said Josh. "But we're not going to start exploiting teens just to get gifts." He stared at the blank paper in front of him. "You think I should script what I'm going to say? I don't want it to be forced."

"Men are men," Azzie said, using his best British accent. "The best sometimes forget."

"Azzie, please tell me you aren't still quoting Shakespeare."

"I can't lie, Josh. It's from Othello." Azzie stared at the ceiling as he thought. "You don't want it to sound scripted, but you also don't want to sound dumb. You gonna ask them for money?"

"Um, yeah," said Joshua, scribbling down a few sentences from the brochure onto his yellow pad. "I was planning on it—I mean, especially if I can find a way of saying like, 'We're so glad Bob has chosen to get involved in our ministry and invest in us.'" Josh pulled his briefcase out from at his feet. "Anyway, you know Bob—he doesn't mess around. I may not even have to ask for anything. He may just say, 'OK, everybody, pony up.'"

"Expectation is the root of all heartache," Azzie quoted in a wistful British accent.

"Azzie, enough Shakespeare. Two quotes in five minutes is like two too many." Josh loaded the brochures and yellow pad in his briefcase. "Look, I have a meeting with the district attorney, and then I'll be in court for a while and then on to Starbucks to work on this presentation, so I won't see you before I leave. Any final words?"

"Ask well," Azzie nodded sagely. "I like a paycheck. And ask if they like scotchmellow cookies. We might have a few left over after tomorrow's cookie run."

"No cookie asks, Az," Josh said with a gentle rebuke. "I'm not doing this for crumbs." He hurried out of the office and headed to see the DA.

After sitting through multiple juvenile hearings, all for teens that he knew from the juvenile detention center Bible study, Josh spent a long afternoon at Starbucks trying to capture his ministry on paper. *If hearing those lawyers cross examining witnesses didn't prepare me to ask for money, I don't know what other preparation there could be.* Two of the teens he saw in court were released back into foster care. Another teen returned to Juvie, and the fourth ended up being tried as an adult for drug dealing to a minor. *That was a hard blow, but not entirely unexpected. The kid ... he's a kid, but he's 17. He should have known better than to try to sell meth—crystal meth at that—at Douglass Elementary. The kids there—we're giving them cookies. They should want cookies, not meth.*

He thought about how to explain it all to a group whom he was pretty sure had never been anywhere near a juvenile court in their life. *I doubt there's going to be a lot of people who want to give money to enable me to befriend a kid who got caught selling meth to elementary school kids.*

Josh tried to push the thoughts out of his head as he crossed over the Willamette River and joined the rest of the city making the late afternoon exodus to the cleaner, safer Westside. *Bob and his wife ... what was her name? Anne? Bob and Anne ... There's no way they'd invite me over if they weren't ready to get their friends behind LLF. Hopefully Bob already bragged to everybody about his going to a birthday party for a juvenile delinquent. He'll probably do most of the talking anyway, knowing full well that everybody there would be scared stiff to do what Bob did. I think that's probably why a lot of people give—so they don't have to get personally involved. Which is fine by me, since if they really knew that we help teenage meth dealers, they'd probably get all self-righteous anyway.* His car barely moved in traffic. He checked his watch, breathing an inward sigh of relief that he'd remembered to allow himself so much extra time.

Brochures and happy stories are much better for this kind of a crowd, anyway. Bob probably runs this group like he runs the rest of everything in his life. If they have even half as much money as Bob does, then we may finally get out from underneath this constant hat-in-hand life we lead.

Five miles and forty minutes later, he pulled onto the lake-front property and parked in a corner of the circular drive.

I can't believe I forgot to wash my car, he mused. *Driving a cheap Honda goes over well with donors. Driving a dirty Honda does not.*

Josh knocked hesitantly at the door and waited for what seemed like an eternity before Bob flung it open.

"Josh Stiller! Glad you could come." He motioned for Josh to follow him deep into the well-appointed home. "Our fellowship group has been doing a series on helping the needy, and since it was meeting at our house tonight, I figured you should come."

Josh tried to pass for casual, seeking not to gawk at the opulence that engulfed him. *How long is this hallway, anyway?*

"Uh, that's a great idea, Bob. So how long have you been doing the study?"

"Well, we started it last week. It's all based around some book about treasures in heaven that the group is supposed to be reading . . . it sounded like what you guys do, so I figured you should be here. We already started, since Anne wanted to do dinner for everyone tonight."

He showed Josh into the living room, where four couples were seated in a casual circle of rich brown leather couches and armchairs, already busy in friendly and casual conversation.

"Folks, I'd like you to meet Josh Stiller." Josh nodded and smiled, giving an especially large smile to Anne, whom he had met once before with Bob at a past LLF banquet at his old church. "He runs a ministry over on the shady side of town—helping kids stay out of trouble and getting their lives back on track. I was there last week. Hard to believe what happens just a few miles away from here." The couples all nodded in agreement.

Bob sat next to Anne and motioned for Josh to take a deep sinking seat into an isolated oversized armchair next to the fireplace at the front of the room. "Josh, why don't you tell everyone what you do?" *Not quite the rousing and detailed personal testimonial and endorsement and call to arms that I was anticipating,* gulped Josh. He self-consciously loosened his tie.

"Um, hi everyone. I'd like to thank you, and especially Bob and Anne, for letting me come tell you about my ministry. It's called Live Life Fully, and like Bob said, we're in the part of town where you probably don't do a lot of your shopping." He laughed nervously.

Flat line, thought Josh. *No response. Somebody throw me a bone.*

"On our side of town, kids have a pretty rough life. We have drug wars, gang problems, street violence, broken homes—all stuff that you hear about on the news."

Because the only crime in Lake Oswego is someone tailgating you, taking your parking spot, or picking some of your flowers, he thought to himself.

"At LFF—that's Live Life Fully—we try to end that cycle. We work with teens, doing Bible studies, mentoring them, meeting with them in juvenile detention, and trying to keep them out of trouble."

Josh shifted his weight, seeking to surface one final time before the armchair finally engulfed him whole.

"The neighborhood really needs our ministry. We're in the northeast section and have the highest crime rate, both of violent and domestic crimes, in Portland—almost more than double the city average."

There's the windup, thought Josh, *and here's the pitch. The ask.* His tongue clung to the roof of his mouth while his tonsils dropped down to meet his heart, which had just informed the rest of his body organs that it would shortly be leaping out of Josh's chest.

"Uh . . . these kids really need your help. Bob and Anne just, uh, made a great gift to, uh, help financially with the ministry, which was, uh, such a blessing because you know these are, uh, tough economic times for our ministry, and, uh, I don't know if Bob told you about coming down and being a part of a birthday party we had for one teen family, but, uh, it was great to have you there, Bob, and, uh, I know not everyone is in a position to come down to an event like that, but, uh, we could really use your prayers and your support, both for our ministry and for our teens, and I understand you've been talking about this kind of thing in your small group, so . . ."

Josh's voice trailed off, perhaps swallowed up by the armchair as well.

They're still not responding. And I may be stuck in this chair for life. He opened his briefcase.

"I brought a brochure about our ministry for each of you, so, uh, let me pass those around here, and, uh, it'll tell you a little bit more about our programs and our approach. I know you can talk to Bob or me if you'd like to know more, so . . . uh . . . Does anyone have any questions about us or what we do or?"

He looked from face to face, all smiling politely and shaking their heads no.

Bob stood up, seeming slightly flustered. "Well, folks, that's Live Life Fully. They're a good example of a ministry that works with the needy." He turned to the fellowship group leader. "Let me go get Josh settled in with some refreshments, if you want to continue the discussion." He motioned for Josh to follow and then shut the doors to the living room behind them.

Josh swallowed nervously as they entered the kitchen. *I have a distinct feeling that Bob's major concern here isn't my hydration level.*

"So, Bob . . . how'd we do?"

"Josh, just what exactly did you have in mind?" Bob asked quietly, though his tone was firm. "Why did you ask for money?"

"I, uh—I'm really sorry, Bob. I think I totally misunderstood what you were thinking about for tonight. I was just thinking based on your excitement and your gift and your coming down last week that you wanted me to kind of give everyone a chance to get involved, and . . ."

"That's exactly what I had in mind, Josh—but that's not what you did."

Well, he's not exactly happy but not exactly spitting nails, thought Josh. *That's good. At least I have only a major problem on my hands as opposed to an absolute catastrophe.*

"I *wanted* you to give them the same kind of opportunity to get involved that you gave me. I wanted you to challenge them—make them uncomfortable—question their stereotypes. But the only opportunities you gave them were giving money to you so you could keep doing the ministry, and then praying for your success." Bob thunked an ice-filled glass down in front of Josh and proceeded to fill it with Diet Coke.

What would I like to drink, you ask? Oh yes, a Diet Coke would be fine, thanks. Josh felt like a stupid kid. He knew Bob was absolutely right, which made it all the worse. He sheepishly guzzled the beverage, avoiding Bob's gaze.

"Josh, every person in this group lives in one of the nicest parts of Portland. I don't normally invite ministries to speak to this group, for fear that they'll do exactly what you did tonight: Speak like they're talking to ATM machines. Tell them how they can buy their way out of getting involved. Encourage them to leave things to the experts! I had you figured as a guy who could get these folks out of their comfort zone, put them in the combat zone, get them to put their faith in action. You let them off the hook and, Josh, you let me down."

"I . . ." Josh leaned back on the kitchen counter, watched the ice clink in the now-empty glass. "Bob, I'm sorry. I feel terrible. You're absolutely right. I got so focused on my needs—the needs of LLF—that I wasn't thinking in terms of challenging anybody to do anything more than write a check."

"Josh," Bob said, gently lifting the glass out of his hand and refilling it. "Giving is all fine and dandy—these folks do it all day long. And everybody knows a ministry needs money to run. But *how can you give to what you don't understand?* And I'm not talking about them understanding what your organization does. And I'm not talking about the kind of understanding that you get in a lecture." He handed the refilled glass back to Josh, who was able to look up at him at last. "I'm talking about the kind of understanding you get when all your easy answers are taken away from you because of what's staring you right in the face."

"Bob, please let me go in and apologize to everybody," Josh offered earnestly. "I don't want my stupidity to reflect poorly onto you."

"Too late for that," Bob laughed, but not at all harshly. "You're already in too deep. Besides, I don't want an apology from you. I want a challenge from you—for them." He poked Josh's chest while Josh was taking a drink. "Look, you never told me about the ministry, Josh. I never took a brochure. You put me in the middle of the mine field and said, 'Let's see which of your preconceived notions survives, you old codger.'"

"I did?" coughed Josh.

"Yeah, you did," Bob was already moving back toward the living room. Josh wanted to stop him, ask him more. He certainly didn't feel ready to re-enter the Room of Doom and sit in the Armchair of No Return. "I got to bring a birthday present for a little girl who hopefully won't repeat her parents' mistakes—because you stepped into her parents' lives. That was why I gave."

"But Bob, how do I get these people involved?"

"Invite them, Josh. It's simple! Throw down the gantlet. Ask them to get in their cars and drive down there and do something. Surely you have something that happens every day, or every week, that they can come see, and touch, and do. Now, come on—let's go." Bob opened the doors to the living room, gesturing for Josh to be the first to pass through.

Sure, thought Josh. *They could come sit in court with me all day and see how messed up some of these kids are. They could meet with our teen dads support group and hear how many problems these guys face for not making their girlfriends abort the kid. They could come to the pre-natal classes for pregnant teens that a volunteer teaches and see the looks on the faces of girls that dropped out of school because the morning sickness was so bad. Or . . . they could see the look on a dad's face the day his baby is born. The look on a mom's face when she brings us her ultrasound pictures. The expressions on their faces when they get their first baby shower gift. The little girl that is healthy because her mother quit smoking. The expressions the day they come into the office and tell us they haven't had a drink or done drugs for a month. The day they get out of Juvie, or the day they get off probation. The day they realize that God loves them.*

Scratch that. Maybe they can sponsor a cookie.

"Bob, I have an idea." Josh stayed away from the open door as if lions were about to spring through it. "Tomorrow—we're doing a massive cookie delivery to the elementary school in our neighborhood. Frederick Douglass. What about if I invite anyone who wants to come? We can always use more volunteers, and they'd get to touch kids' lives."

"Cookie delivery?" Bob smiled. "That didn't make your brochure."

"Oh, the brochures are a few ye . . . never mind. It's something new. We just started it a few weeks ago. Most of these kids come from homes where their parents won't make them cookies—either because they don't know how, or they're too dysfunctional, or they're latchkey kids, or whatever. We think that each kid should have someone who cares enough about him or her to bring a warm cookie to school—and so we deliver cookies, personally, to each kid, once a week."

Bob rolled his eyes. "Josh, why on earth didn't you say that ten minutes ago instead of your salesman shpiel? Most of these ladies work from home so they can be home with their kids—or make cookies for their kids. They would love to help with that. They could see what you do and get their toe in the water. Now come on . . ." He grabbed Josh's shirt sleeve and marched him back into the living room.

The most painful feeling Josh experienced the rest of the evening was the residual effect of being poked in the chest by Bob. Soon he was back out in his unwashed Honda on the still-busy freeway. He dialed Azariah on his cell phone. "Azzie?"

"Hey, J! How'd the meeting go? Are we rolling in cash money, man?"

"Azzie, you were right."

"Man, that's almost never good. And that always means no cash money. How was I right?"

"Expectation is the root of all disappointment."

Azzie paused. "This is one time where I wish Shakespeare was wrong. How bad was it?"

"Well, that's the funny part. It was bad—I mean, really, really bad. But it turned out to be the good kind of bad that ends really well, only without any money."

"Josh, did someone drop you on your head? You're not making any sense, man."

"Probably just hunger, Az," said Josh, exiting off the freeway where traffic was still averaging thirty miles per hour. "Apparently I showed up after dinner. How do you feel about me crashing at your place for half an hour? I really don't feel like sitting in traffic for another hour to get to my house."

"Sure. And you're in luck: I'm reheating chili."

"Azzie, we need to find you a girlfriend. Chili is not the base of the food pyramid."

Ten minutes later, Josh was comfortably situated on a well-worn couch in Azzie's apartment, cupping a bowl of chili. "How did the teen dads group go?"

"It was okay. We got a new member. His name is Jeremy . . . new kid in the neighborhood. He managed to get a girl pregnant within six months of moving here. His girlfriend knows Shiana, and Shiana told her to tell him to come see us or get dumped . . . so he did. He's a tough cookie, but I think he might turn out. He's just enough of a cross be-tween a love-sick puppy and a womanizer to care that his girlfriend told him to shape up or ship out."

"It's definitely been a day of tough cookies and shipping out," grunted Josh between mouthfuls.

"Bob's got a bunch of toughies in his fellowship group?" Azzie asked, refilling his own bowl. "Are they all grouchy like him?"

"Hardly. They were very polite: They politely listened and then politely ignored me. At first, anyway."

"And then you showed them that picture of me holding my bounced check at the bank and they all melted, right?" Azzie struck up a pitiful pose with an imaginary check.

"Yeah, that's it," Josh chuckled. "Actually, I struck out in Round One of my presentation—the part where I talked about us and our needs. Then Bob gave me the hook into the kitchen and beat me senseless."

"For real?" Azzie cocked his head.

"Yeah, pretty much. My chest still has a hole in it from where he put his finger through it. But I deserved it, Az. You were right. Bob was right. Bob said the same thing you did: Challenge people to get involved. Get them doing something. Get them baking cookies or making cookies or delivering cookies. I used to think we were in the youth ministry business, but these days I feel more like Mrs. Fields."

The two smiled and ate in silence for a minute before Josh continued.

"Bob spoke about giving almost like it was something that rich people did when they *didn't* care and *didn't* want to get involved." Josh set the empty bowl on the coffee table. "I've always sensed that, you know? Like there were two kinds of giving: giving to get people off your back—or giving out of guilt, or giving just because someone asked you to—and then a second kind of giving that you can do only after you really care about something deeply."

"That would change fundraising strategy a little," Azzie mused.

"How so?" asked Josh.

Azzie stroked his chin thoughtfully. "Right now, when we meet someone who has money, we kind of act like they're a major donor waiting to be convinced that we're the ministry that's the most deserving of it. Like it's a contest or something, and they're just trying to figure out who to write the check to. But maybe it's not about us. Maybe you can win the beauty contest and lose the check."

"Maybe you're right, Az. Maybe the worst thing a person can say about LLF is, 'Man, you guys are great; I couldn't do what you do.' Because what they really mean when they say that is, 'And I'm not going to do what you do; it might as well be happening on another planet, because it sure isn't a part of my life.'" Josh stretched his legs out on the coffee table. "So people have to learn how to give *as a result of* their involvement? Is that what I'm hearing?"

"Makes sense, J," nodded Azariah, adding his legs to the coffee table. "Heart first, treasure second. And to get the heart these days, you got to get more than the brain. You got to get the arms moving and the eyes seeing and the legs walking." He looked around his apartment. "Too bad we don't have a whiteboard around here."

Josh fished a wadded-up LLF brochure out of his pocket. "I think we just found a good use for our brochures," he said, reaching in his other pocket for a pen. "Scratch paper."

"So what's the *Question of the Moment*, boss?"

"Well, let's see," pondered Josh. "Donors are made, not born—I guess that's what we're saying. And these days they're born out of involvement in the cause, not knowledge of the organization and how great it is."

Josh turned the brochure sideways and used his best scribbling to write the *Question of the Moment*: "What if . . . giving is something you learn (in the midst of your personal involvement), not something you are born with (that's activated by your awareness)?"

"An excellent question, Sherlock Homeboy, and I think you may have learned the answer today," Azzie responded. "People have to learn how to give with their arms and legs before they can truly give from their hearts. Maybe the cookie delivery tomorrow will teach people's arms and legs how to give. If nothing else, it can't hurt . . . unless they don't show up. That could hurt."

"Let's not think about that. I'd like to end on an epiphany." Josh capped his pen. "Giving is learned. On that note, I'm going home."

QUESTION OF THE MOMENT

1. What if the relationship between donors is as important as the relationship between the donor and our ministry?

2. What if the donor is the primary way of spreading the shared cause within his or her network?

3. What if . . . fundraising is a result of equipping ordinary people to solve the problems we solve and share the cause we love?

4. What if . . . giving is something you learn (in the midst of your personal involvement), not something you are born with (that's activated by your awareness)?"

To Ponder

1. Think back to your last meeting with a donor or potential donor, or your last presentation. What would your audience say was the primary focus? Given Josh's experience and learning in this chapter, what would you do differently now?

2. When you have an opportunity to meet with high net worth individuals, do you approach that meeting differently than you would approach a meeting with a volunteer? In what ways? Why or why not?

3. If giving is not about convincing people to give to you instead of somewhere else, but more about teaching them to give in the first place, what are three techniques, tools or activities you presently use that you would stop using or change? Why? What are three new techniques, tools, or activities that you could adopt?

4. Josh describes two kinds of giving: "giving to get people off your back—or giving out of guilt, or giving just because someone asked you to—and then a second kind of giving that you can do only after you really care about something deeply." Do you have personal experiences of each type of giving in your own life? How about in your own ministry? Describe those experiences.

5. Azzie says, ". . . to get the heart these days, you got to get more than the brain. You got to get the arms moving and the eyes seeing and the legs walking." Consider your public presentation and the materials you use. What senses *must* a person use to engage with those materials? How could you adapt your materials so that the audience was *required* to get their arms moving, eyes seeing, and legs walking as a part of your actual initial presentation?

Chapter 5

Josh was back in the office a few minutes after eight Tuesday morning, picking up the work that wasn't finished Monday and trying to prepare for a massive cookie distribution that might or might not include major donors.

Azzie came in the door a few minutes later. "Josh, I had an epiphany after you left."

Josh looked up from his work. "About the major donors that may or may not be coming for Operation Cookie Delivery?"

"Yes . . . no . . . well, sort of. More about people learning to give and learning to get involved. Here's what I was thinking." Azzie planted his feet almost as if he were about to toss up a free throw. "Those of us who 'give' to the ministry and own it more than anyone else. We weren't born that way. We had to *learn* how to give and get passionate about this ministry, right?"

"Right?" Josh answered cautiously.

Azzie took a step forward. "Each of us needs to learn how to give by getting involved. So somebody's got to teach us. What if we were to go back and figure out how *we* got involved and learned to give, and then we tried to take other people through the same process?"

Josh narrowed his eyes thoughtfully and rubbed his chin. "Reverse engineer ourselves, in other words. Interesting, Azzie. I like it."

"I like it enough to try it on us. What were some of the experiences God took you through that ultimately landed you in that chair?"

"Hmm . . ." Josh leaned back, hands behind his head, staring off into distant memories. "Well, it's not like I grew up in this neighborhood—I grew up in safe, quiet, suburban Sacramento. We didn't have the same problems there."

"So how did you hear about the problems?" queried Azzie, assuming the position of whiteboard scribe.

"Honestly? I moved to Portland and drove into the wrong part of town and ended up totally lost. In the ten minutes I was driving around—which was like a block away from here—I saw like two drug deals and some gang members shaking down a couple of middle school kids. It totally blew my mind . . . and not like pot does." Josh shook his head, old memories surfacing. "I knew I had to do something, but I didn't really know what. At first, I got my church to try doing stuff like coming down here to clean up graffiti. And then we did the old Christmas presents for needy families thing, but I just felt like we weren't getting anywhere. The graffiti would reappear like five minutes after we left, and it's almost like you have to stand in line to give away Christmas presents to needy families sometimes, you know? Because everybody's doing it. That and turkeys at Thanksgiving."

They both laughed in recognition of the truth of what Josh was saying. Azzie still hadn't written anything down on the white board but remained poised to strike.

"I dunno," said Josh, slumping forward, elbows on desk. "It just never felt like we were reaching the deeper issues. You could give these kids Nintendos at Christmas and still see in their eyes that they had zero hope in their lives . . . so I figured that if the love and hope of God was needed by anyone in the city, they needed it. I had this feeling that somebody should be getting to the heart of the problems, and since there wasn't a ministry, I . . ."

"Started your own ministry?" Azzie offered.

"Actually, I got dared into doing it," Josh said, chuckling. "I was talking to the pastor at a church around here—too bad the guy isn't in the neighborhood anymore, actually—and he said that if I found a hole that needed to be filled, it was because God was going to use me to fill it."

"So what did your wife say?" asked Azzie.

"Oh, she totally agreed. Which at the time I didn't really think about how weird that was that she would support the idea, but now like every day I think, 'What was she thinking?' Yeah, Beth is great." Josh smiled at the picture of his wife on his desk, appreciating her anew and forgetting momentarily about Azariah's question.

"Josh, come on—the marker fumes are affecting my ability to remember Shakespeare!" Azzie waved his hand in front of his face.

"Oh, sorry. Right." Josh intentionally paused before snapping back to attention. "Yeah, so Beth and I started coming down here every few days to meet with teens and start building relationships with the families in the neighborhood. After about six months, we both knew this was where God wanted us. I guess we both just had this God-sense that He wanted us to be in the neighborhood—be a part of it."

He looked up at Azzie. "Did I ever tell you that we bought the closest funeral-plot-masquerading-as-a-home to this neighborhood that we could find? It was kind of our way of saying to God, 'We're serious. We're here to stay.' Try diagramming *that* on a white board!"

Azzie drew two tiny tombstones and turned back toward Josh. "Like that?"

"I guess there was no lightning bolt in the sky that got me here." Josh stood up from his desk and walked over to Azzie and the white board. "It really was a step-by-step process—definitely had to be God. I definitely didn't plan to start a ministry."

Josh started counting on his fingers as Azzie wrote on the board. "First, I had to actually see the need. I didn't even know it existed. You hear about the drug deals and shootings, but only as statistics. Once you see middle schoolers getting pulled into gang wars and elementary school kids getting drugs shoved at them, or six-year-olds walking around because no one is home to take care of them, I don't think you can go back, you know? You can't forget that . . . you have to do something. It was kind of like going on a mission trip, except this one was across town."

Azzie nodded. "It was the same for me at Moody—I thought *this* neighborhood was bad, and then I moved there. It was like seeing the future of my neighborhood—if somebody didn't step up and start changing things. Like it would be dangerous for anybody except gang bangers to live here. I didn't want that for my nieces and nephews and stuff."

"So we both saw a need," mused Josh, staring at the board. "I saw how different, how bad it was, and you saw what it would become if nobody did anything."

"But I don't think we just jumped into action," Azzie noted. "I mean, we saw the need, but you had someone pushing you to do something, and I had someone pushing me to do something."

Josh nodded. "I saw it, but I didn't—couldn't—do anything for a few years, really. I didn't know *what* to do, or where to do it. It wasn't until I talked to that pastor who lived here—who saw the problems every day—that I figured out how I could help. I needed someone to *show* me how to get involved before I got involved."

Azzie wrote "involvement" on the white board. "So were you ready to give at that point?"

Josh paused.

I wasn't giving. Does that mean I wasn't ready? Or just didn't know where to give? "I suppose I wasn't ready. If someone had asked me to give, honestly? I wouldn't have. Because all the giving I had seen people do hadn't changed anything. I wanted to get in there and roll up my sleeves . . ."

". . . just like Lois does," interrupted Azariah. "Just like Bob does."

Oh, thought Josh. *Light bulb moment.*

Josh wondered what he would have done if he had walked through the doors of LLF ten years ago and the executive director asked him to fold newsletters. *The weird thing is that I probably would have done it. And I probably would have*

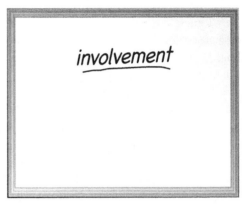

thought, *"That's about right for me, because I really don't have a lot of experience, and . . . whatever."*

That's just like Lois, thought Josh. *So I'm not so different from them after all. We felt the same thing. . . .the difference is that now there's an organization. They don't have to start something new. They can just hop onto the ministry we have.*

"Except we're the ones who own the organization," concluded Josh out loud. "Not legally, I mean—it's a nonprofit—but in terms of deciding who gets to do what, we own it. It's our baby."

"So you think Lois feels any different?" asked Azzie. "That cookie project is her baby. *She* owns it— just try telling her to change her recipe. Maybe she . . . and Bob . . . and others . . . want to own the ministry like we do," Azzie suggested.

"So . . . is giving owning?" Josh asked, pushing himself up to sit on his desk. "Can people give without owning the cause?"

"Well, yeah," said Azzie tentatively. "Like you were saying, some people give just to get *out* of owning the cause. I mean, look at all the donors we have who don't even participate with the ministry. They'd freak out if somebody handed them a cookie tray and a map to Douglass."

Josh cocked his head to one side, then hopped up in a flash of inspiration. He took the white board pen, drawing a line under his latest *Question of the Moment.*

"Azzie, Lois is right: Somebody doesn't become a major donor when they donate a certain amount of money to an organization. Somebody becomes a major donor when they get their friends to give their lives to tackle a cause."

"So . . . Lois really *is* a major donor!" Azzie shook his head, grinning.

"I'll tell her eventually. Right now . . ." Josh started writing. *What if donors are categorized by their involvement and ownership of the ministry, rather than the number of zeros on their check?*

"Josh, what if it isn't the ministry?" Azzie ventured. "Remember how both Lois and Bob . . . and we . . . were invested in the cause of helping youth, even before we knew about the ministry? The ministry was just the tool to get us there." He took the pen and changed *ministry* to *shared cause.* "That's a little more consistent with what our volunteers . . . donors . . . major donors have been telling us."

"I think you're right. They're committed to helping hurting teens, and we just happen to be there to help them help others."

"Speaking of," added Azzie, "Lois said she was going to bake an extra few dozen cookies for today, just because things were so popular last time . . . but she'll need to get people to start donating baking supplies, or money for them, because Social Security and food stamps only go so far."

Josh nodded again. "If anyone shows up today, I might just throw out cookie sponsorship as an option."

"And if I eat as many cookies as I did last time," said Azzie, "I might just throw up as an option!"

Lois arrived a few hours later with an army of volunteers and enough cookies to feed two armies of students. Her Crown Victoria, extra spacious due to the shredded seats and stolen stereo, was stuffed full of warm cookies. A few other cars had boxes of cookies steaming up the windows, but none of the cars in the caravan looked like the ones Josh saw in Bob's driveway the night before.

Josh kept waiting. *Maybe they didn't estimate the amount of time it would take to get across town. Maybe they got lost like I did that first time . . .*

Azzie stood by the door, obviously eager to head out. "Josh, the cookies are cooling off, and I can sample only so many before Lois gets cranky. Are you ready?"

Josh grabbed his coat reluctantly and followed them out.

They drove a few blocks to the elementary school, meeting the principal while Josh scanned the parking lot expectantly. *I don't see anyone who looks out of place for the neighborhood. Looks like no cookie sponsorships for today.*

Ten minutes into the cookie stampede of youth, Josh noticed someone talking to Lois. *She definitely doesn't belong in this neighborhood . . . wasn't she one of the ladies from Bob and Anne's fellowship group? I should meet her . . .*

Lois immediately turned to Josh as he approached the conversation. "Josh, this is Jean. She said Bob invited her to come."

Josh nodded and held out his hand. "Jean, I'm very glad you could come. Has Lois been telling you all about the cookie delivery?"

"Oh, not yet," Jean said, glancing at Lois. "I just got here. I got really, really lost."

Josh smiled.

"But she did just let me sample one of the cookies," laughed Jean. "I think I'd like to be on the receiving end . . . but giving is just as good, and a little easier on my hips."

Jean took a box of cookies and joined Josh as he handed out cookies down rows of school cafeteria tables.

"Last night you mentioned that you just started this cookie ministry a couple of weeks ago," Jean said, in between children leaping up like cookie piranhas. "What on earth gave you the idea to start a cookie delivery program? I assumed you would be doing street preaching and passing out tracts to high schoolers."

"Lois was actually the one who started the program, Jean," said Josh, fighting off cookie piranhas of his own. "Came up with the idea and everything. She had lots of cookies left over from a bake sale she had done for us, and all of the sudden she was just gripped by this thought that every kid should have a warm cookie."

Josh's box was now empty. "I know it sounds kind of funny, but that warm cookie actually represents something of the spirit of Live Life Fully." He playfully set the empty box on the head of one of the kids who was happily munching on a scotchmellow. "We're trying to break the cycle of dysfunction that these kids live in, and a cookie is a very tangible way to fill one of the gaps in their life."

Jean showed a mixture of interest and skepticism. "But don't you wonder if it's really doing anything long-term? Or does it just give them a sugar buzz?"

"Honestly? We're not sure yet," Josh answered, shrugging. "But we think it will help us connect with these kids—give us a chance to show them that we care." Josh looked thoughtfully across the tables filled with children. "And whatever the long-term consequences, I'd rather have them hooked on home-made scotchmellow cookies from Grandma Lois than on whatever candy the corner drug dealer happens to be doling out."

They continued talking as they finished delivering all the cookies, dispersing almost as quickly as they gathered.

Josh was ecstatic by the time he returned to the office. "Azzie, did you get a chance to meet Jean?"

"Yeah. I handed her off to Lois when she came in . . . I really didn't know who she was."

"She," said Josh, leaning down into Azariah's face, "was one of the people from the fellowship group last night. I invited her, and she came."

He retreated to his desk, doing his best to appear nonchalant. "She asked an interesting question. I hadn't thought about it before, but . . . well, it was interesting. And convicting."

"Was it, 'Why don't you pay your support staff better?'" Azzie teased.

"Hardly," chuckled Josh. "Right after we finished passing out all the cookies, she asked why I presented the way I did last night at Bob's house."

Azzie frowned. "Didn't you just do a normal presentation?"

"Well, that's just it," replied Josh, leaning back in his chair. "I did a normal presentation—at least up through the point that Bob took me into the kitchen and put a hole in my chest. But I didn't tell her that. I just said, 'Well, that's kind of our normal presentation.' So her next question was why it was so normal. I told her we needed money to continue the ministry."

"So she disagreed? Did she change her mind after being here today?" asked Azzie.

"No, that's just it," said Josh, leaning forward and drumming his index fingers on his desk pensively. "She said that coming down here made her even more convinced that God is using us—which is good, of course—but it also convinced her all the more that we shouldn't be telling people that we need money."

Azzie rolled his eyes. "For real? Man, that's so Westside!"

"That's what I thought at first, too, but she put me in my place. See, she's all for us talking about people *giving*. What she said was that . . ." Josh paused to recall. *What were her exact words?* "She said, 'God wants you to be in ministry, so quit telling people you'll go out of ministry if they don't give. You make it sound like God won't be faithful to his servants.'"

"Ouch," Azzie winced. "She pulls no punches . . . Worse than Bob and Lois put together."

"Right, I know . . . but I think it hurt the most because she was *right*." Josh punctuated the thought with a gentle slap of his palms on the desk. He pushed himself up from the chair and strode over to the white board. He almost felt like he was about to make a presentation, only of a very different kind.

"See, we've been moaning to everyone we meet about not making payroll, or being under budget, or getting paid with cookies—not exactly things that express a confidence that God will provide. I've been thinking about it since she said it."

Josh could feel a head of steam developing from somewhere inside him as he talked faster and a bit louder. "Even in churches these days, half of the pastors act like it's a virtue to not talk about giving." Josh continued. "They hide the offering plates and only talk about stewardship right before they mail out the budget commitment cards."

Josh continued. "If Christians aren't regularly telling the world about the faithfulness and generosity of God, then who will? Scripture says, 'And God will provide your need in Christ Jesus.' But that's not what we write in our newsletters. *We* write, 'Well, God didn't provide our need in Christ Jesus, so you had better pony up!'"

"If we keep telling people month after month that God hasn't been faithful to meet our need to do the ministry he called us to, what kind of an effect does that have over time? And if you get a zillion nonprofits telling Christians the same thing month after month, how in the world can we expect Christians to be eager to give?"

Azzie frowned thoughtfully. "That makes sense. But, well . . . if God *has* been providing for us, why are we always broke?"

Josh smacked his fist into his hand. "*Great* question, Azzie! It's the same question I was asking on the way back here from Douglass! I was praying, 'OK, God, if you're so good at providing, why am I always having to go out begging? And in a voice that was almost like He was sitting right next to me in the car, I heard Him say, 'Well, how long has Lois been sitting in your office folding newsletters?'"

"That's deep," whistled Azzie. "So you're saying we missed God because we were looking for cash money, and God was trying to send us something better . . ."

". . . yeah, the rest of the team that God was trying to put in place to do the job!" Josh interrupted, breathless. "And with that team—as we developed them and stretched them and challenged them—would come the cash money that the whole team needed to operate!"

"Seek first the Kingdom of God . . ." started Azzie.

". . . and then God throws the cash money in as a bonus!" finished Josh. "How cool is that?"

Azzie nodded, processing it all. He paused for a moment in silence, watching Josh turn toward the white board and uncap a marker. "Except for one question: If we tell people God will provide . . . then why would *they* provide?"

Josh's marker halted in midair. *That's the kicker,* thought Josh. *Do I tell them that God plans to provide . . . through them? That's kind of presumptuous. And how would I even know if that's true? Or do I tell them that God will provide, whether they give or not? Isn't that what Mordecai says to Esther in the Book of Esther? "For if you remain silent at this time, relief and deliverance for the Jews will arise from another place . . ." Or would that let them off the hook? Maybe that's why Mordecai finishes his sentence with, ". . . but you and your father's family will perish."*

"Maybe . . ." Josh said aloud at last. "Maybe it has to do with Jesus' saying that 'It is better to give than receive.' Jean mentioned that jokingly today. She said giving cookies away tasted even better than eating them. If we apply that to giving money . . ."

Josh poised his marker to write but wasn't sure what.

"That's it!" Azzie interrupted. "We've been missing the point all along. The point of getting people involved and getting them to give. It's not about us surviving. If God is faithful—and we know that He is—then the donors donating isn't the point at all. The point is *to grow the donor* . . . because then everyone wins!"

Josh turned toward Azzie and pursed his lips. "Now I'm not tracking, Azzie. Grow the donor? Into what?"

"Grow into giving . . . grow into serving . . . grow the donor into being what Jesus Christ intended them to be all along. Hold up a second." Azzie grabbed the Bible from the satchel leaning against his desk and rummaged through the pages. "Ok, got it, and it isn't Shakespeare. It's from Ephesians chapter 4: 'It was he who gave some to be apostles, some to be prophets, some to be evangelists, and some to be pastors and teachers.' That would be us, right?"

"Right," replied Josh, intrigued.

"But," continued Azariah, "It *doesn't* go on to say, ' . . . and he gave these pastors and teachers and evangelists lots of supporters for their ministry.'" He pointed the Bible toward Josh. "Here's what it says: 'It was he who gave some to be apostles, some to be prophets, some to be evangelists, and some to be pastors and teachers *to prepare God's people for works of service . . .'*"

". . . 'so that the body of Christ may be built up . . . ' I remember this now, yeah," said Josh, moving toward Azariah.

". . . 'until we all reach unity in the faith and in the knowledge of the Son of God,'" continued Azariah, "'and become *mature*, attaining to the whole measure of the fullness of Christ.' Here, take a look." He handed the Bible to Josh, who continued to read silently:

> *Then we will no longer be infants, tossed back and forth by the waves, and blown here and there by every wind of teaching and by the cunning and craftiness of men in their deceitful scheming. Instead, speaking the truth in love, we will in all things grow up into him who is the Head, that is, Christ. From him the whole body, joined and held together by every supporting ligament, grows and builds itself up in love, as each part does its work.*

Josh stopped reading. *It is time*, he thought, *to stop being tossed back and forth by the waves.*

Azzie rose from the desk and headed to the white board. "This is what we've been dancing around all along. Giving isn't born in donors. They have to grow into it." He uncapped the pen. "The point of them giving is for us to help bring them to a place where they're serving God with everything they've got, including their money."

"And the point of getting them involved is so they can have their lives impacted just as much as they impact other people's lives," added Josh. "Like with Bob after he came to the party. Next time I saw him, he didn't seem to be nearly as much of a grouch—even when I blew up his whole Bible study."

"He was changed . . . in a *one-hour birthday party*." whispered Azzie. "Why? Because he got to change someone else's life." Azzie drew an arrow to Josh's musings on faithfulness and fundraising. "This is the piece that makes it fit together. We tell people about the faithfulness of God, give them a chance to experience it by diving in. Then they get to live in service to God." He capped the pen. "That's even better than getting a tax-deductible receipt, man."

"So our fundraising . . ." Josh returned to the *Question of the Moment* board, picking up a pen of his own. "*What if . . . fundraising activities . . . no, that isn't it.*" He erased it. "*What if donor development is first and foremost a statement about the faithfulness of God?*"

"Josh, this is brilliant. This is revolutionary." Azzie was talking faster and faster as he got more excited. "What am I doing putting donors in these Excel spreadsheets according to how big a check they wrote? We got to *not* group them by check size any more, man. We got to group them by their *growth*. We got to track their growth in Jesus Christ through our ministry! Our ministry is just the tool—the vessel—for them to grow."

Josh nodded enthusiastically. "That's what Lois and Bob—and now Jean—have been trying to get us to do. They're all growing in Christ, in different ways. They're all at different points, and they each need to grow in different ways. And the weird thing is that they kind of know it!"

"They all have different levels of involvement. They have gone through different steps of connection, just like we did, to bring them to the point where they're now at." Josh gave up writing and started pacing, gesturing like a Latin American evangelist as he talked. "We went through steps of involvement to bring us toward maturity in Jesus Christ. The ministry, LLF, was one step along the way. It was the vessel. Now, we're in a position where we can use LLF as a tool for teens and donors. As donors grow in Christ, they can serve the teens that so desperately need Christ. It's like two sides of a coin!"

"So now what's our goal? To move donors through a transformational process that will cause them growth." Azzie shook his head. "Wow. That's quite a change from where we were a few weeks ago." He pointed to the *Question of the Moment* board. "How are we ever going to explain this one, or implement it?"

"Let's . . . let's try it on Jean and Bob. They're willing guinea pigs, except they don't know it yet. I think they'll be the perfect candidates." Josh rubbed his hands excitedly. "I feel like the light bulb really just came on. Ten years of fundraising, and it's actually starting to be exciting."

QUESTION OF THE MOMENT

1. What if the relationship between donors is as important as the relationship between the donor and our ministry?

2. What if the donor is the primary way of spreading the shared cause within his or her network?

3. What if . . . fundraising is a result of equipping ordinary people to solve the problems we solve and share the cause we love?

4. What if . . . giving is something you learn (in the midst of your personal involvement), not something you are born with (that's activated by your awareness)?"

5. What if donors are categorized by their involvement and ownership of the shared cause, rather than the number of zeros on their check?

6. What if donor development is first and foremost a statement about the faithfulness of God?

To Ponder

1. What are the steps God took you through that brought you to your current role with your organization? How did you get involved? When did you start giving? When did you start spreading the cause? How much of this shapes the way you disciple your donors? How might it more fully shape your donor discipleship process?

2. Josh says, "Somebody doesn't become a major donor when they donate a certain amount of money to an organization. Somebody becomes a major donor when they get their friends to give their lives to tackle a cause." Who is on your major donor list now that does not fit that definition? Who is not currently on your list who does?

3. Does your fundraising program express a confidence that God will provide? How? In what ways might your program send a message that God's provision is not reliable?

4. What in the world did Jesus *really* mean when He said, "It is better to give than receive"? Does that apply to your donor discipleship efforts as well? In what way is it better for you to give to your donors than to receive from them?

5. Is your fundraising program currently structured so that your donors are supporters for you, or so that you are a supporter for your donors, equipping them to personally tackle the cause you share with them? What is the most a donor could grow in this way through your donor discipleship program?

Chapter 6

A little more than three weeks had elapsed since Josh's appearance at Bob's party and Jean's subsequent participation in the cookie delivery at Frederick Douglass Elementary. Bob's gift had made it possible for Josh's thoughts and Outlook calendar to drift away from donor calls and fundraising plans and back to the regular parade of court visits, teen small group meetings, and one-on-one counseling sessions that typified life at LLF.

Lois's efforts had continued unabated, but her oversight and ownership of the deliveries were so complete that Josh had chosen to do little more than wave and smile and offer bits of innocuous encouragement to the stream of volunteers gathering at the LLF office before cookie runs. Josh had noted wryly to himself that seniors brandishing cookie trays were now almost as common a sight at LLF as teens with court-ordered tracking bracelets. But that was about all he had noted about donors until, on Thursday, he was updating his task list in Outlook and noted a new item that had just turned red:

NEWSLETTER COPY DUE

Copy due already? Josh groaned, remembering that the previous month his volunteer artist had threatened to "*really* quit this time, Josh, if you give me the text late again. I don't do this for you out of the staggering potential for professional advancement, you know."

Right, right—I know, thought Josh, noting that artists required about as much attention and pampering as donors to keep them happy. *Teens don't mess up their lives on your schedule, you know,* he mentally retorted to the artist. *And cookies for kids are great, but I don't see any of these cookie grandmas fielding calls from lockup at 3 AM.*

Josh caught his thoughts darkening. *Alright—pity party's over. It's newsletter time.*

"Young Azariah," he called in a troubadour voice to his companion in the desk across from him. "Stop whatever you are doing, and sound the newsletter horn. It is time for us to summon our inner muses and create yet another masterpiece. Our adoring public awaits."

Azzie slumped a bit as he continued to update small group attendance sheets on his computer. "Okay, J . . ." he intoned slowly, not looking up from the screen. "You go ahead and get started, and I'll join you when I'm done here in, uh, just another day or two."

"Nice try, Az," said Josh, swiveling up and out of his chair and striding over to Azariah's desk with his laptop. "This, however, is an equal opportunity for all of us to experience the pain of the dentist's office without anyone even sticking a hand in your mouth. C'mon now. Get your muse on." He opened a blank Word document.

"Say, J," said Azzie, turning away from his own screen reluctantly. "Weren't you and I supposed to have a meeting on how we could redo the newsletter and turn it into a donor discipleship tool? Part of a whole donor discipleship communications strategy? This ringing a bell?"

Josh frowned. "Shoot. You're right." He drummed his fingers on the palmrest of his laptop. Sometimes thinking about donor discipleship seemed like a chore. Other times it seemed like a bottomless pit. Always it felt like something that got in the way of the ministry he wanted to do. He liked the theories he and Azzie had begun to develop weeks before, but really putting them into practice? It seemed like the kind of thing he'd have the time or energy to do only if some truly major donor made a truly major gift that would free up truly major amounts of his time as his office dripped with staff answering to his every beck and whim.

"I don't know, Az," he sighed. "We're already close to being late. Maybe this time we just . . ."

"It doesn't have to be a perfect donor discipleship newsletter, man," interrupted Azariah gently, in a rare moment of correction. "All we got to do is move it one step farther along the road."

Josh surrendered a smile. "One step farther along the road. You're right, Az. You're right." He rubbed his chin thoughtfully. "So what did we do last time in the newsletter that we can move one step further along? Remind me . . . I tend to block traumatic events entirely out of my conscious memory."

"Well, lessee . . ." mused Azzie, rubbing his chin in reply. "Last time we had Lois in here *folding* the newsletters, so . . ."

". . . so if we took one step farther along the road . . ." intoned Josh, leaning forward.

". . . we'd have Lois *write* the newsletter!" the two shouted in unison, high fiving each other and collapsing back into their chairs in laughter.

"I love me this donor discipleship work," said Azzie, shaking his head in satisfaction.

"Donors gotta own the cause," affirmed Josh in reply. He had already pulled his cell phone off his hip and was dialing Lois's number. Azzie waited in eager expectation.

"Lois! Josh here. Where are you now?" Josh nodded to Azzie. "Then keep on coming in, because there's a newsletter planning meeting going on, and you're already late!" He leaned forward to return a fist bump from Azzie. "Yeah, I'm serious, Lois. We need to keep taking steps forward in donor discipleship. Last month you folded the newsletters. This month your story goes above the fold." He paused, signaling a thumbs up to Azzie. "You got it. Your scribes are at the ready. See you in five minutes."

Azzie snapped forward in his chair. "You serious? She said yes?"

Josh nodded, raising his hands to frame an imaginary headline. "'Cookie Ministry Enables Widow to Live Life Fully.' Now if *that's* not a step forward . . ."

The two passed the next ten minutes in happy silence, Azzie entering data and Josh checking emails with his laptop wedged between legs propped up on Azzie's desk.

Lois walked into the office and knocked on the doorframe. "Is this the editorial desk?"

Josh set his laptop down and popped up to hug her. "The very place, Miss G'ma Lois Newsletter Editor Cookie Baker Volunteer Extraordinaire. Let me pull you up a chair. Azzie and I were just warming up the keyboard in preparation for you."

"Oh, and G, check these out." Azzie pulled a sheaf of digital photo printouts from his desk drawer and handed them to Lois. "Photos from that last cookie delivery Josh and I were at."

Josh looked over Lois's shoulder as she flipped through the pages. "Now see, *that's* a great cover photo there. Little headline like 'Cookie Ministry Enables Widow to Live Life Fully.' Little text about how the bake sale flop became the cookie delivery success, how to volunteer, voila: Page 1 is *Layoutsville*."

Lois peered back over her shoulder at Josh. "Page *2* is done, you mean. We've got business to take care of on Page 1."

Josh and Azzie exchanged puzzled glances.

"You *gotta* talk about the Cookie Ministry on Page 1, Lois," urged Josh, continuing to look at Azzie.

"Right, G," affirmed Azzie, sitting back down as Lois eased into the chair Josh had pulled up next to his own. "That's the biggest news we've had around here in months. And you're the ringleader. Ette. Ringleaderette."

Josh frowned at him and watched as Lois paid them no mind, scooting his laptop over to rest right in front of her. He had no idea Lois had ever used a computer before. As he watched her, he realized his initial diagnosis was correct: she stared hard at the keyboard, locating each key and giving it a deliberate tap, clearly thinking twice before each motion so as to avoid making an error.

"This . . ." read Josh. Azzie, curious, stood up and took his place next to Josh, reading over Lois's other shoulder as she typed.

"This Month's . . ."

"This Month's *Obituary* . . ." Lois's typing continued unabated.

"This Month's Obituary? Are you *crazy*, Lois?" Josh slapped his hands against his thighs and walked a resigned figure eight around the small office. "Where's the cookie story? The feel good story . . . The pictures of the little kids and the cute grandmas and the cookie sponsorship ask . . ." His voice trailed off.

"This Month's Obituary," Azzie continued. "Kevin Jackson."

Kevin Jackson. The name settled thickly into Josh's chest. Kevin Jackson was a dropout who had been a runner for years. Small time, low level operator. Dime baggies of marijuana. Crack cut with Ajax. Junk stuff. Didn't even have a nickname. *Always wearing headphones, hat pulled down to his collar. Never said anything to anybody. Never had an expression on his face. Even when he shot himself in the stomach in that stupid gun play accident. His death wasn't front page news,* scoffed Josh. *And now Lois wants to what—lionize the guy on the front page of our newsletter?*

"Lois," sighed Josh. "Kevin Jackson was a punk. A thug. No LLF donor in their right mind is gonna feel sorry for this guy. Sold black rock to homeless bums. Probably already gave cheap reefer to half the kids you're giving cookies to at Douglass. Blows a hole through his own intestines when he was reaching in his pocket to make change for three high school kids buying date rape drugs? This is not the stuff of Hallmark dramas, Lois."

Josh was the only figure moving in the room. Azzie stayed riveted to the screen while Lois continued to type. Eventually Josh came to rest back at Lois's shoulder, reading what Lois wrote.

This Month's Obituary: Kevin Jackson
by Lois Randall

Kevin Jackson was a pusher. He died this month of a self-inflicted gunshot wound while dealing drugs to three teenagers. Kevin was 19. For the last five years of his life Kevin made a living getting young people hooked on drugs. He never showed an ounce of pity to anyone, and is never recorded to have engaged in an act of compassion. He will not be remembered for acts of bravery or sacrifice. As he rolled through the neighborhood in his beat up sedan, bass shaking windows as he passed, his facial expression never changed. It was a mixture of contempt and disinterest.

It was the same expression that remained on his face when I visited the funeral home during the viewing. His grandmother was the only other person there. She stood in front of the casket looking somber and weak. Not knowing what to ask, I simply stood next to her. Not knowing what to say, I found myself unable to leave.

Many minutes passed. At last his grandmother spoke. "I would have given my life for his," she said conclusively. I nodded.

It was a preposterous thought from a clearly longsuffering woman. Kevin likely would have been more than content to have made the trade—her life for his. And he would have rolled away in his sedan, face betraying contempt and disinterest as the bass shook the windows as he'd pass, on the way to his next drug deal.

Her life for his. An absolutely foolish transaction.

But what about my life *and* her life for his? And what about my life *and* her life *and* your life?

Funny how the more lives that are offered in sacrifice for one, the fewer people who end up dead.

There is an old saying, "Many hands make light work." Hands can hold other hands that mourn. Hands can bake cookies. Hands can teach and train and invest time in those who otherwise will be forgotten. In short, many hands can do the simple things that are described in the pages that follow in this newsletter.

But one hand alone? In this neighborhood? It is always in danger of shooting the young body it's attached to.

So as long as I'm permitted to do so, I intend to put one obituary from this neighborhood on the cover of this newsletter each month until I can convince you that the cost of sitting on your hands is much greater than the cost of lending your hands to the efforts described herein.

Please use your hand to turn the page now and learn of the simple ways that people just like you are using to keep kids like Kevin from ending up on the covers of newsletters like this.

"Dang," said Azzie slowly and appreciatively. "Cookie delivery *is* Page 2."

"Dang is right," added Josh, squeezing Lois's shoulder gently. "Lois, that's amazing."

"Josh," announced Lois resolutely, facing the keyboard still, fingers poised to type. "I think it's time for us to start a gang."

"A *what?*" Josh's brain, having already moved on to the safety of Page 2 and cookie deliveries, was jarred back to the present by Lois's pronouncement.

"A gang," she repeated flatly. "You know: Mongols. Puddle Cutters. Paso Robles Boyz. Eighteenth Street. CVS. A gang."

Josh choked. "Whatever happened . . . happened . . . to cookie deliveries?"

"A perfectly good gang initiation," affirmed Lois. "But our work is Live Life Fully, is it not? And cookie deliveries alone can't save a neighborhood."

Our own gang? Saving a neighborhood? Josh's mind whirled, hanging on the precipice of thinking that what Lois was proposing was absolutely crazy, but not altogether sure he didn't want to jump in, too. Suddenly the whiteboard conversations he'd previously had with Azzie seemed a lot less theoretical.

"Lois—a *gang*? That's a serious word to mess with—a serious *world* to mess with."

"Seven-year-olds and ten-years-olds mess with it every day in this neighborhood, Josh," countered Lois. "The neighborhood has dozens of bad gangs and not one good gang."

Our own gang?

"We'll never root out gangs from this neighborhood, Josh," continued Lois. "There will always be parents here who neglect their kids. Like anywhere else, kids here are looking for a place to belong." She pushed back her chair, moved the laptop to the side, and sat on Azzie's desk facing them both.

"But look at what you have the opportunity to do." She narrowed her eyes and looked intently at them both. "LLF is already a gang. It has its own rituals and rules and initiations. It undoes the things that the bad gangs do. It cleans up graffiti instead of tagging every building it sees. It gets kids out of Juvie instead of in. It provides structure and meaning and a sense of purpose to young people. Ergo, gang."

"Problem is," she continued, leaning back and crossing her arms, "it's a pretty poorly organized gang. Always getting kicked around by other gangs and skulking away back to its building. But why?"

She looked intently at Josh and then at Azzie. "It's already got members all over Portland. Its members have far more money and far more influence than Eighteenth Street. It can recruit folks from anywhere in this city. Mow a few of its members down; ten more will take the place of each one. *Many hands make light work*, Josh. It's how you win. Do it just like the big gangs do. They get kids started young, tagging. But they don't just leave them as taggers. They train them up, become runners. And the black and Asian gangs in Portland? They've moved on to organized crime." Lois paused briefly.

"So start . . ." she said, sliding up off the desk, "with cookie deliveries. But don't end there. Overwhelm this neighborhood with the LLF Gang presence. Twenty-four hours a day, seven days a week. Let them job-shadow you. Introduce them to a teen that needs mentoring. Have them lead singing and story time at Juvie. Invite them to a birthday party for Naomi, or whoever has a birthday party. Charge them dues."

She gently poked Josh in the chest, right where Bob had. "In other words, Josh," she challenged, "You already have a gang, Josh. *Man up and run it*. And put that in the newsletter."

She walked through Azzie and Josh and began to head out the door. Turning to face them one last time, she added sweetly, "I can't wait to see the newsletter, boys. Should I come by next Friday to stuff them?"

"Uh . . . Friday works, yeah."

Josh rubbed the back of his head absent-mindedly. "See you . . . Lois."

Lois offered a final wave and departed, leaving Josh and Azzie staring at her wake.

"What just happened, Az?" muttered Josh, not taking his eyes off the doorway.

"Lois just moved things a step forward, J," Azzie replied, remaining as transfixed as Josh. "She just went from donor to owner."

"So do we head over to the laptop for newsletter Page 2 or over to the whiteboard for LLF Page 2?"

Azzie turned to face Josh. "Whiteboard," he nodded. "Definitely whiteboard."

The two scrambled to retrieve markers and whiteboard and assemble their chairs around it, reviewing what they had written weeks before and beginning to talk . . . about Lois, Bob, Jean, Kevin, gangs, LLF, and how it all fit together. They spoke of a turning point—a sense that things had changed and would no longer be the same, and how that that was both exciting and bittersweet.

"Okay, so let's think it through this way," resolved Josh, turning to the whiteboard and sketching out three columns:

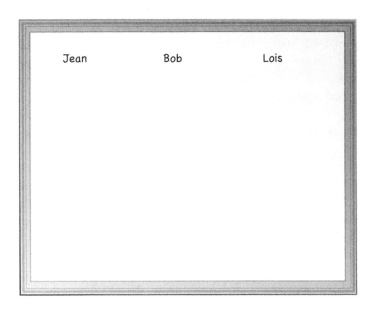

Jean   Bob   Lois

"The way I see it," said Josh, tidying up a crooked line, "is that Jean, Bob, and Lois are clearly each at different stages in their relationship with LLF. And the weird thing is," he continued, tapping the middle third of the board, "that in our old system of doing development, we would have said that *Bob* was the top of the heap—the major donor—because of his sizeable gift. But it's pretty clear by what we've seen from Lois in the last month . . ."

". . . and the last five minutes . . ." added Azzie.

". . . yeah, exactly . . . that Lois is further along than Bob. She's obviously having a more major impact on LLF than any of the other donors."

"And we couldn't even really call Jean a 'donor' because she hasn't given any kind of a gift," noted Azzie.

"Right," nodded Josh. "But in our old system we would call her something like a 'potential donor,' which doesn't seem to fit, because she's already participating in the ministry. But calling her a 'volunteer' doesn't seem to fit either, because she's obviously grappling with the thought of making a gift based on her involvement." Josh rubbed his chin. "Somehow calling her a 'volunteer-slash-potential high net worth major donor' seems clumsy, and like we're missing the point. Not to mention, it's something that would insult her if she heard us using the term."

"And," Azzie tapped the third segment of the board, "we used to think of Lois as 'our best volunteer' who also gave a regular donation each month. But when it came to donor categories, we just thought of her as a 'regular' donor because her donation was so small."

Azzie rubbed his chin. "Ain't no way Lois is a regular anything."

Josh frowned. "It's almost like the vocabulary we use—'volunteer,' 'regular donor,' 'major donor'—causes us to fail to see each person's true potential relative to LLF and how to maximize that."

"Or see what God is doing in their life and how to come alongside them and help them grow," mused Azzie.

"Oh, thank *you,* Mr. Spiritual, for making me look like a total fundraising hack!" Josh laughed, smacking Azzie playfully on the back of the head.

"Watch the marker on the 'fro, man," Azzie waved his arms around his head in mock protest. "But I'm serious, J—I mean, look at the deal with Bob."

"Which deal is that?"

"He grew up with no help from us, J," explained Azzie. "It's like it happened by accident, but it could have happened on purpose. One day he was here participating in a birthday party—by accident—and next thing you know, he's got you over at his house speaking to a group about troubled teens, and he's like totally engaged with the cause."

"Hmm . . ." Josh narrowed his eyes. "It's like there are these projects—cookie delivery, birthday parties, folding newsletters—that people start with. And then if the projects fire them up, they want to go deeper."

"Hey, check this out, J," exclaimed Azzie, borrowing the marker out of Josh's hand.

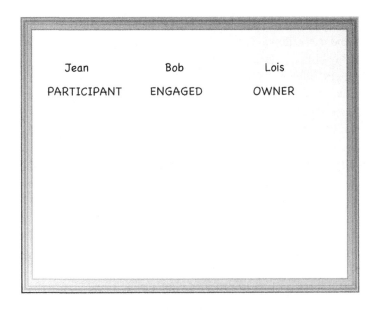

Jean	Bob	Lois
PARTICIPANT	ENGAGED	OWNER

"Dang!" whistled Josh. "That's good!"

"And you could even call Jean a 'participant' to her face and she wouldn't hate on you," noted Azzie.

"Right," Josh replied reflectively. "And it's interesting how some participants kind of move on naturally without us doing anything—like Bob—but other participants are probably gonna stay where they're at unless we nudge them along to maximize their potential—like Jean."

"Come alongside them prayerfully to help disciple them, yeah," nodded Azzie, continuing to look at the board. Josh glanced over at him and shook his head, chuckling.

"Duly corrected, Mr. Ministry. Now checkity check *this* out." Josh snatched the marker back from Azzie.

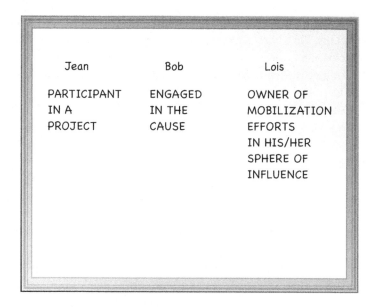

Jean	Bob	Lois
PARTICIPANT IN A PROJECT	ENGAGED IN THE CAUSE	OWNER OF MOBILIZATION EFFORTS IN HIS/HER SPHERE OF INFLUENCE

"Not bad, J. Not bad," nodded Azzie, grinning broadly. He paused and cocked his head to one side. "But here's my question, J: Isn't Bob owning the mobilization effort in his sphere of influence? I mean, he had you over to his house. Even gave you a Diet Coke, man."

Josh smacked his fist into his palm. "Aha! I was waiting for you to ask that!" He rubbed his hands together. "You know what I realized is the difference between Bob and Lois?" Azzie shrugged, palms turned up. "Bob got his friends together . . . *and called me over* to talk to them about troubled teens. Lois? She calls everybody herself."

"Now *that's* good!" Azzie concluded, pointing to Josh with both index fingers.

". . . because for someone at the engagement level, it's the most logical thing in the world to call in the 'expert', right? But once someone's at the ownership level, they're like, 'Get out of the way, fool! I'm comin' through!'"

The two men laughed and exchanged fist bumps.

"You know what I think, J?" continued Azzie at last, turning back toward the board and crossing his arms. "I think there are *good* participation projects and *not so good* participation projects. Like a good participation project is one that gives you a taste of the action, you know? High impact. High touch." Azzie nodded at his own thinking. "You get a person participating in a project like that and you got a lot better chance of getting them engaged."

Josh gestured back toward his laptop on Azzie's desk. "Well, like look at Lois. For *almost ten years* we had her *folding newsletters.* That's a participation project, but you'd hardly call it high impact."

"But give the woman a batch of cookies," added Azzie, "and she's on the O-train!"

"O-train?" puzzled Josh.

"You know, Ownership," replied Azzie. "P-E-O. Participation-Engagement-Ownership. And," he added. "LLF is like the tracks the train runs on. It ain't the train!"

"Now *that's* the million dollar insight right there!" affirmed Josh. "Uh, I mean *that's* the deeply moving spiritual revelation," he corrected himself, glancing sidelong at Azzie.

"See, because at each stop along the way," continued Azzie, "the train needs different things from the, uh, track, there, and . . ."

Josh squeezed Azzie's shoulder. "I think your train analogy just broke down there, Casey Jones. But your thinking is absolutely on the right track: What Jean needs from us is different than what Bob needs from us is different than what Lois needs from us. Like so." Josh started writing again.

"Dang, J!" exclaimed Azzie, laughing. "Where did you *get* that?"

"Hey, you're not the only super spiritual person in the room here, Az," chuckled Josh. "Years of picking up the check at failed donor lunches has to have prepared me for something, right?"

"Well, that 'hungry for engagement' part fits in perfectly with the cookie ministry. No doubt. But the whole thing still needs a title."

"Hmm . . ." mused Josh, taking a step back to survey the whiteboard in total. "How about 'Donor Discipleship'?"

"Could freak out folks like Jean," pondered Azzie. "They might think the whole 'participate' thing is just bait and switch so they open their wallets."

"Ah, right. True, true," nodded Josh. "How about Supporter? Backer? Ministry advocate? Growee? Disciple? Winner?"

"How about 'None of the above'?" Azzie strode over to his desk and pulled up the thesaurus on his computer.

"What? You don't like 'Growee'?" whimpered Josh, feigning hurt feelings.

"J—wait—what about this: 'Champion'."

Josh stood quietly.

Champion.

As in "championing a cause."

As in that one Psalm where it says, "Like a champion rejoicing to run his course."
Yeah.
Champion.
"Champion it is, Az," pronounced Josh. Over the top of the chart on the whiteboard he wrote:

How LLF Coaches Champions

Azzie joined Josh in standing before the whiteboard, transfixed. "You know the weird thing, J?" whispered Azzie. "In the old system, major donors supported organizations. But in this new system, organizations support their champions."

Josh turned to face Azzie with newfound appreciation.

How LLF Coaches Champions

P	E	O
<u>Jean</u>	<u>Bob</u>	<u>Lois</u>
PARTICIPANT IN PROJECT	ENGAGED IN THE CAUSE	OWNER OF MOBILIZATION EFFORTS IN HIS/HER SPHERE OF INFLUENCE
LLF serves as a project host with projects that are short-term, high-impact, high-touch, easy to understand, and likely to make a participant hungry for engagement.	LLF serves as an ongoing discussion partner, giving opportunities to understand and engage with the cause at a deeper and deeper level.	LLF serves as a supporter and accountability partner, providing tools, coaching, and accountability.

To Ponder

1. For LLF, taking one step forward meant they had Lois write their newsletter. What one step could you take *today* with one donor that would move you away from fundraising and towards coaching champions?

2. Josh perpetually sees LLF as being short of major donors, yet Lois tells Josh, "You already have a gang, Josh. Man up and run it." What about your ministry? How would you respond to the statement, "God has already supplied everyone you need to succeed with your cause"? How might you, like Josh, be overlooking vast resources which God has already supplied to you?

3. The cookie ministry is a "signature" participation project for LLF—something very unique that distinguishes LLF from other causes (unlike a golf scramble, a bake sale, or a jog-a-thon). Does your ministry have a signature participation project that provides an easy entry point into your ministry? If so, how does it rate when evaluated according to the criteria Josh and Azzie identify in this chapter, and how can you improve it? If not, brainstorm at least three possible participation project ideas that might work for your ministry. Use the criteria in this chapter to evaluate their potential effectiveness.

4. Think through your list of donors and potential donors according to the new Coaching Champions strategy that Josh and Azzie discuss in this chapter. Which three individuals would be Participants? Engaged? Owners? Who did you formerly classify as a "major donor" or "volunteer" who would be classified very differently within this new system?

5. Azzie discovers that within this new system, the organization's job is to help its major donors champion the cause in their spheres of influence, not the other way around. In what ways are you supporting and equipping your major donors to champion the cause rather than simply support you as you champion the cause? What one new thing could you start doing to reverse the traditional support equation?

Chapter 7

"Dude . . . I'm a cookie," Azzie proclaimed. He made a slightly sheepish face when two chuckles from the other room indicated both Lois and Mary Ellen had heard him from their newsletter stuffing stations.

Josh glanced up from his desk to see Azzie hovering over with a plate of snickerdoodles.

Azzie continued, a little quieter this time. "You said it yourself the other day—we want more O's for our cause. We called it 'coaching champions,' right? So, how do we get more O's?"

Josh's eyes returned to the email he had been writing. "Uh, that's the million dollar question, isn't it?"

"Then get your checkbook ready, because here's the answer. You ask Betty Crocker."

"What?" Josh replied suspiciously.

"I told you . . . I'm a cookie, man." Azzie nodded at the snickerdoodles on the plate he was holding. "I think O's are cookies, and we have to find the recipe to make them. You know, each cookie might be a little different, but I bet the basic ingredients are the same."

"I think all that sugar has gone to your head, Az . . . but I'm sort of catching on to what you're saying. I hadn't given much thought to you and me being O's, but I guess we are. I guess I'm a cookie, too."

"Right on, J!" affirmed Azzie. "So the way I see it, what we really should do is start by figuring out what an O looks like . . . figuring out our cookie recipe . . . and then maybe we can see what ingredients we need to make some more."

"You know, Az, that actually makes a lot of sense. To the whiteboard, then!" Josh said theatrically.

"I'll bring the cookies."

Azzie continued as they broke out the markers. "So, if we want to make O's, our goal should be to come up with a recipe that helps transform people into mature followers of Jesus Christ—as it relates to our cause."

What Makes Us O's?

RELATING – personal relationships with teens

PRAYING – praying for teens and the neighborhood

SERVING – meeting needs of teens

SHARING – spreading the cause wherever we can

GIVING – actively giving to cause

HEALING – experienced some type of redemption or healing
as it relates to teens (personal or someone else)

"Wait—did you just call us 'mature'?" Josh replied as he beamed a Nerf ball right at Azzie's head.

"Only for the sake of argument. Let's just say we're mature in Jesus Christ as it relates to the cause of helping teens in this neighborhood, at least compared to most people. But that's cool. It's like Paul tells Timothy, 'You heard me do it, and you saw me do it. Now go teach others to do it, too.'"

"You know, Az, only you can find a link between cookies and the words of Paul," chided Josh.

"So," blushed Azzie, "now we need to come up with the ingredients . . . or the steps . . . through which we need to lead people so they can reach their full potential."

Jumping up and seizing the marker, Josh said "So, if Lois, you and I are the O's at LLF, what do we do that makes us O's?"

"Well, we all have personal relationships with needy or at-risk teens."

"Okay, good. So, relationships . . . relating. What else?"

"Lois is a real prayer warrior. And you and I regularly pray for the kids we work with."

"So, praying."

Josh continued as he wrote "Serving" on the board. "What about this? The three of us each do things to meet the needs of teens in our community."

"I think I'm finally catching on to this 'ing' thing," mused Azzie. "How about sharing . . . as in, we all share and spread the cause wherever and whenever we can? Oh—and where does 'giving' fit? Is it a totally separate category?"

"Yeah, I think it is." As Josh wrote it in, he mused, "Taking our cookie metaphor one step too far . . . maybe it's the leavening agent."

The two surveyed the board, Josh tapping the marker next to each entry he had written.

"Okay," he summarized, "so we have relating, praying, serving, sharing, and giving. Is that it?"

Azzie's eyes narrowed like he was trying to read something far away. "I don't know. It seems like there still needs to be something a bit more, um, intangible added in there. Secret ingredient, y'know."

After a long pause, Azzie continued. "Check this out, J: Haven't the three of us each experienced some healing or redemption in our relationships either *as* teens or *with* teens? Like for me, I experienced the healing firsthand when you helped me get my life straight. With Lois, she saw it when you helped her grandson get back on track. So how do you write that out as a category?"

"Healing?" asked Josh. "Actually, I like it just the way you said it. Healing works for me."

They paused for a moment, admiring the board which now read:

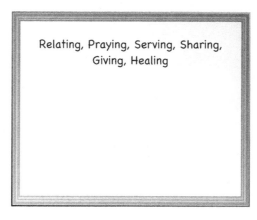

Relating, Praying, Serving, Sharing, Giving, Healing

"These are the categories we can use to disciple our champions," announced Josh. He paused. "Do you realize how Live Life Fully just changed? We're not just helping youth anymore. We're helping champions live fully for Jesus Christ so that *they* can help youth live fully."

Azzie shook his head. "Dang, that's cool. It's like God had that planned all along . . . we just took a while to catch up with Him."

The men looked at each other and then chimed in unison, "We need Lois."

After surveying the board and hearing the excited explanation, Lois said, "Makes sense, boys. So what next? What do we do to make more people like us?"

Josh and Azzie exchanged puzzled glances. "Uh . . . " Josh mumbled. "That's why you're here, Lois."

They all stared at the board blankly for a minute. Then Lois erased the whole thing and drew this:

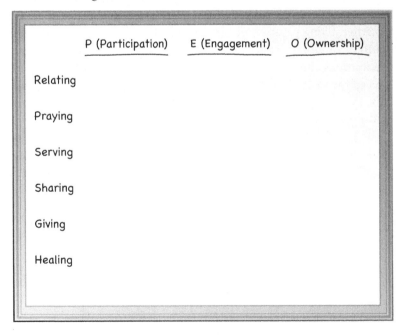

	P (Participation)	E (Engagement)	O (Ownership)
Relating			
Praying			
Serving			
Sharing			
Giving			
Healing			

"It seems like we need to have opportunities in each of the categories at each of the levels," she ventured. "And our goal would be to help each person move forward in each area, not just one."

She folded her arms and regarded the board thoughtfully. "So, for example," she continued, "a P activity for praying might be for a champion to come to one of the annual Pray for Our City events. And an E might host one Pray for Our City event at their church. And maybe an O would promote the events to other churches. See what I mean?"

A clearly impressed Azzie replied, "Lois, you rock. That's brilliant!"

Josh's brain was already on a roll. "So, let's look at the things we do and see where they fit. The cookie ministry. Definitely a good opportunity to get new people involved, so it's a P, right? I think that lands in 'Serving' since we're meeting a need?"

Lois wrote "cookie ministry" in the P box next to "Serving" and surrendered her marker to Azzie. "You guys take it from here. That newsletter won't stuff itself."

Azzie watched her go, obviously thinking something. "About that newsletter, J," he mused. "Stuffing the newsletter is a good 'Sharing' activity, right? But, writing the newsletter—that's got to be at the O level of 'Sharing,' I'm thinking."

"What about birthday parties or baby showers?" Josh added. "I could see that as serving, since we're meeting a need. But I think it is more about developing relationships with the kids we serve. So, let's put those under 'Relating.' In the P, let's put 'attending a baby shower.' But, under E, could we put 'hosting a baby shower'? Would that make sense?"

"Does to me," replied Azzie.

"And what else do we do?" Josh twirled the marker in the air as if it would stir up thoughts that might be floating around. "We've got this new gang idea. Where would that fit? Joining the gang would probably be at the E level—engaged. That would be 'Serving.'"

"You know what doesn't fit here, J?" offered Azzie. "Bake sales. No wonder they were a bust. They didn't help transform people and they had nothing to do with our cause."

They continued filling in the boxes with the lists of all the ways people could be involved with LLF—Bible studies, visits to Juvie, and so on.

After surveying the board, Azzie said "We still have some serious gaps, J. No wonder we don't have many O's. We haven't been adding the right ingredients to the recipe."

"But it's not like we have time to start thirty new initiatives," Josh protested. "We're running as fast as we can."

"True, true," nodded Azzie. "But it's just like we talked about when we had Lois write the newsletter, man. All we have to do is take one step. What one thing could we do?" He put his finger on the E category. "We could start with Bob. What would be the next step in Bob's path toward becoming a LLF champion?"

	P (Participation)	E (Engagement)	O (Ownership)
Relating	Attending a baby shower	Hosting a baby shower Visiting teens in Juvie Mentoring a teen	
Praying	Attending a Pray for Our City event	Host a Pray for Our City event at church or ???	Promote Pray for Our City events to local churches
Serving	Baking or handing out cookies	Join an LLF gang	Lead an LLF gang
Sharing	Stuffing newsletters		Helping write newsletter
Giving	Donating items for baby showers		
Healing			

Josh rubbed his chin, then snapped his fingers together. "Here's a wild idea," he announced. "Let's ask Bob! He's stopping by and we're going to lunch. Let's ask him what he'd like to do next."

"What, no streamers this time?" Bob teased as he entered the office.

"What, no check this time?" Josh replied, wincing almost immediately as he said it. *That* was *funny*, he thought. *Funny enough to get me killed.*

Josh extended his hand, glad that Bob didn't seem to notice his impertinence. *There are advantages to working with the self-centered,* thought Josh. "Bob, welcome. Come on back. I have something to share with you."

After Josh's initial explanation of the P-E-O discovery, he searched Bob's face anxiously. *Is he offended? Confused?*

"Something's missing here, Josh," frowned Bob. "This is big on theory, but what are you going to *do* with the information?"

Josh opened his mouth to say something, but shut it for fear that something foolish would sneak out again. He was relieved when Bob continued.

Bob continued, "What if you worked to develop individual plans to help people move through the steps? Someone like me isn't going to bake cookies, but I might be able to mentor a teen who is interested in law . . . something like that."

Did he really just tell us the next step he wants to take? Is it really that easy?

"It's like basic sales," concluded Bob. "Except you don't have to hide it from people. You aren't tricking them. You're helping them. Actually, it is kind of refreshing."

"What do you mean?" quizzed Josh.

"Well, let's chart a plan for Jean." He grabbed the marker and started writing. "She ended up coming to your cookie delivery, right?"

Funny how everyone feels free to grab the marker, mused Josh.

"So, she's already 'serving' at the P level. So, what could she do to begin 'Relating'— getting to know the teens we serve?"

Did he just say "we"?

Azzie interjected, "Baby showers. She could attend a baby shower."

"Bingo!" roared Bob joyfully, jabbing Azzie in the chest with the marker. "And then, if that really suits her, you could ask her to host one—thereby moving her from P to E."

Azzie clutched his chest while Josh smirked. "And after that," Azzie said, still in obvious pain, "she could begin inviting her friends to the showers and encouraging them to get involved. She'd make more P's."

Worried that Azzie was still clutching his chest, Josh looked at the clock and interjected, "Bob, we better get going to lunch."

As they walked out, Josh cupped Bob's elbow. "Bob—what you said about mentoring one of the teens. Were you really serious about that?"

"I don't have time to blow smoke," was the gruff reply.

When Josh returned from lunch, he found Azzie at the whiteboard deep in thought.

"What's up, Az?"

"Just thinking is all," mused Azzie. "We've been talking about getting people to become owners like that's the whole recipe. Like at that point we just eat 'em instead of helping them to keep growing. But O's gotta grow, too, right? But how?"

"Give them more ownership," Josh carelessly suggested, surveying his email inbox. "After all, they're owners, right? So give them responsibility. Instead of us running the project, equip them to run the project. We did it with Lois and the cookies. Let's find another person and equip him or her to run the teen Bible studies."

Azzie nodded, pursing his lips in thought. "I'm sure there's a Josh Junior out there who would love to do that. Find someone who is passionate about a project, and then let 'em own it."

"And share it with all their friends," Josh added, banging on the keyboard to tap out a quick email reply. "They get to walk their friends through the same steps that they went through."

Josh looked up, as if struck by what he had just said. "That would actually have been kind of exciting for me, as I think about it. I would have loved to have drawn more friends into this, instead of doing the Lone Ranger thing, riding into the inner city to save broken youth on my own."

Azzie grimaced. "I ain't no Tonto, Kemosabe."

Josh chuckled and returned to his email. Azzie continued to stare at the board.

"So we need to equip people to begin the participation process with their friends."

Azzie jotted that on the whiteboard, pressing a bit harder with the pen to compensate for the drying ink. "I think we need to invest a little more into our participation projects—especially the gang. I think the gang is Lois's best idea yet."

"And that says a lot from the man who's lived on scotchmellows for the last month," chuckled Josh. He looked up expecting to see Azzie smiling in reply, but was surprised to see his coworker continuing to stare intently at the board. *This champion development process is developing one more champion in this room,* he mused.

"I started dreaming last night about the gang, J," announced Azzie, turning to face Josh with an earnest expression. "You know how the gangs have initiations? And the initiations are different for each person, depending on what the person is most afraid of? We get to do that, except base it on what the person is most interested in. Like, if the person has a passion for helping teen moms, her initiation would be to attend a baby shower and bring a gift. If it's drug recovery, let him spend some time visiting with the recovery group you have, or helping in the detox facility with us at Juvie."

Azzie sat down in the chair in front of Josh's desk. "I think this idea is money, J. I want to see it go."

Josh stared intently and proudly at Azzie. "You're serious about this, aren't you?" he said, searching Azzie's face. "You really want us to do a full-on LLF gang."

"Dude!" Azzie leapt back up, "When the news hears that some Christian organization formed its own gang and is doing initiations and jumping people in and cleaning up the neighborhood and help-ing teens and handing out cookies—all the Kevin Jacksons within six miles of this place will *freak out.* We might even get front page in the metro section!"

Azzie strode back over to the board and stared at it again. "If we could get churches to start their own gangs, or groups—like Bob's fel-lowship group—to get initiated, we could have so many things going on. Remember what Lois said? *Many hands make light work.* It's how we win, man. It's how we *win.*"

Josh slowly caught up with Azzie's enthusiasm. "Az, you're talking about a signature project for LLF—something totally unique, some-thing no one who heard about it would forget."

"That's right," answered Azzie. "A signature participation project for LLF." He wrote SPP on the whiteboard. "A gang of champions. All initiated by us. Living Life Fully in Christ so they can teach teens in this neighborhood what that means."

LLF GANGS—
Signature Participation
Project (SPP)

A gang of champions—
Living Life Fully in Christ so
they can teach teens in this
neighborhood what that means.

Azzie spun toward Josh abruptly. "But let me ask you something serious, J." He paused, gathering up his thought. "Do you think Lois is living life fully in Christ?"

Josh frowned. "What do you mean, Az? She's the one who set up the chart. Of course she's living life fully. She's like the perfect champion for LLF. She jumps in and owns things. She holds us accountable. What is she missing?"

"I thought you might ask me that," answered Azzie slowly. "And I don't mean to say anything bad in the least about the lady who just turned our entire ministry upside down just the way it needed. I think she challenged us in a good way, and now I think she needs us to challenge her back. Or rather," he corrected himself, "I think her family needs us to challenge her back."

"About what?" queried Josh, puzzled.

"J, think about why Lois is part of LLF."

"Well, that's an easy one," said Josh, leaning forward in his chair and placing his chin on his clasped hands. "I worked with her grandson."

"That's right, J—*you* worked with her grandson." Azzie leaned forward, copying Josh's posture. "And you worked with *one* of her grandsons. And every time she's stuffing newsletters, she mentions her *other* grandsons and granddaughters that are still out in the game," said Azzie, softly but intently. "What does it mean that Lois is an O at LLF but a P in her own family?"

Josh stared back at Azzie for what felt to Josh like minutes.

He's right. He's right. He's absolutely right. I've seen it and just tried to ignore it. I've always thought, "What business do I have to butt into her personal life?" But if what this P/E/O process of champion building is all about is mutual accountability relationships that grow us in Jesus Christ? Then that's exactly the business I need to be in.

Josh smiled and looked away from Azzie. *It was easier when all I had to do was to laugh at a major donor's jokes . . . remember their kids' birthdays . . . beg them from time to time.*

He stopped himself.

But none of that changed anything. Didn't change LLF. Didn't change me. And it certainly didn't grow donors—champions, I mean—into the likeness of Christ.

He sighed, steeled his resolve. He'd have to talk to Lois. Because if Lois was going to be the best example she could be, there *was* a way Josh could help her grow.

"So what does it mean, Azzie?" Josh offered at last, addressing Azzie's prior question. "It means I should leave you alone with the whiteboard more often, dear brother and fellow cookie of mine."

To Ponder

1. Think of the O's for your organization (don't forget to include yourself). What are the common ingredients that make you O's? What do you do? How do you interact with those you serve? How do you keep up-to-date on issues relevant to your cause? How do you spread the cause? Okay, now try to turn those into statements ending in "ing" (like relating, sharing, etc.).
2. Discuss those common ingredients with another O from your organization. Does he or she see anything missing? Something that shouldn't be there?
3. Enter your "ing" statements (common ingredients) on a worksheet like this:

	P	E	O
—*ing*			
—*ing*			
—*ing*			
—*ing*			
—*ing*			

Now begin plotting out involvement opportunities you already provide. Where do they fit in this model? Are there opportunities you provide that no longer fit anywhere? Should you still be doing those?

4. Practice developing an individual donor plan for someone currently at the P-level. What is the next logical step? The one after that? Now try an E. Then an O. Does it work? Are there gaps where you need new opportunities or options? What is one opportunity you could add that would make a big impact?
5. Think of one of your organization's O's (owners). In what way should he or she be challenged to grow in relation to your shared cause?

Chapter 8

"**J**osh—what are you doing here?"

Josh turned around to see Bob coming up the courthouse steps. "Oh, hi, Bob! Fancy running into you here." He extended his hand to greet Bob. "One of the kids we've been working with got picked up on an assault charge. I just wanted to be there for him." Bob grunted and frowned. "Josh, from what I know of LLF you have plenty of kids back at the office who are actually serious about turning their lives around." He poked Josh in the chest. "I'd recommend you focus on *those* kids instead of wasting your time with the ones who only call you when they end up here."

"I totally understand what you're saying, Bob," affirmed Josh, sounding more defensive than he intended. "But I think sometimes it takes a few times before a kid really gets it right, you know? And there's nothing like a holding cell for creating a captive audience," Josh chuckled, trying to inject a note of levity. Bob always intimidated him.

"Josh," sighed Bob heavily. "You're smarter than that. If you're always chasing after kids, they'll put no value on you and what you have to offer." He shook his head. "This isn't some after-school special, Josh. Don't be naïve. Focus on the kids who are really working to change."

After-school special? Josh fumed. "Now wait a second, Bob—what if Jesus said that? I'm here because Omar used his one call to call me. I think that means something . . . "

"I think you know better than to fall for a foxhole confession— that's what I think," interrupted Bob.

Foxhole confession? Josh could feel his face go flush. "Bob, look," Josh protested, looking away sourly, "LLF doesn't give up on these kids. They've had people giving up on them their whole lives and I won't add my name to that list . . . even if that means I get taken advantage of a few times. I mean, what if Jesus gave up on us when we messed up?"

Bob looked at Josh with the same penetrating gaze he used when the two were standing in Bob's kitchen some time back. *"Duped."* He enunciated the word with obvious distaste. "You're getting *duped.*"

Josh swallowed hard. "It's a kid's *life*, Bob," he said in a low tone, jaw clenched. "It's not a court case."

Bob was quiet for a second, his gaze never wavering. "I have a hearing in 10 minutes," he said at last, proceeding up the steps past Josh.

A wave of panic washed over Josh.

What did I just do?

"Crisis planning meeting . . . my office," proclaimed Josh as he strode purposefully through the door of LLF.

Azzie followed quickly. "What's up with Omar? Is there more to the story? Was this his third strike?"

"No," sighed Josh, crashing into his seat in defeat. "But I think I just lost us our biggest donor."

"Who, Lois?" Azzie offered incredulously.

"No, our *real* biggest donor . . . Bob." Josh shook his head, staring through the window as if back in time to watch he and Bob on the courthouse steps. "I just ran into Bob at the courthouse. I told him about the situation with Omar, and he said I was being naïve. 'Duped,' he said. So I really laid into him. I may have even raised my voice."

Josh rubbed his eyes and spoke through hands cupped over his face. "He caught me off-guard. I was in ministry-mode, not fundraising mode. You know how defensive I am of these kids. I should have been more careful."

"Well, maybe it wasn't that bad," replied Azzie. "A lot of times Bob doesn't even listen when other people say something."

"Oh, he listened all right," sputtered Josh, recalling Bob's penetrating gaze "Az, I even gave him the 'what if Jesus gave up on us' speech." Josh sighed and shook his head. "Seriously, I think the well just dried up."

"The well?" mused Azzie quietly.

"Maybe I should call and apologize," said Josh, thinking out loud.

"Apologize?" queried Azzie. "For what?"

"For being rude."

Azzie cocked his head. "So were you rude or were you just honest?"

"Doesn't matter," replied Josh in a voice heavy with resignation. "You can't be *that* kind of honest with a donor."

They sat in silence for a half minute, until Azzie began chuckling.

"This is not funny, Az."

"No, I know, I know," replied Azzie, obviously still amused.

"Then why are you still laughing?" demanded a curious Josh.

Azzie nodded toward the whiteboard. "We fell off the whiteboard, J." He chuckled. "Now we're talking about dry wells and donors and fundraising mode and stuff."

Josh raised his eyebrows.

"If it's all about getting The Big Gift, J, then you messed up royally today," Azzie concluded. "But on the P-E-O scale, you just hit one out of the park!"

Josh rose up from the desk and joined Azzie at the whiteboard. "What are you talking about, Az?" he asked, a smidgen of hope creeping into his quiet voice.

"Well, think about it like this, J." Azzie gestured across the breadth of the whiteboard. "In our P-E-O chart, giving big gifts is just one of the ingredients to help grow Bob into an owner of LLF. Big gifts are kinda like the chocolate chips, right? But you can't have a cookie without flour and sugar—and some heat from the oven."

"So you're saying the conversation today was like the heat from the oven, huh?" mused Josh.

"Well, it sure wasn't the sugar," chuckled Azzie. "Sugar's like when you laugh at the donor's jokes and send cards on their birthday. Every cookie needs some sugar, but even when you're trying to make sugar cookies, there's such a thing as too much sugar."

"But when there's too *much* heat," countered Josh, "you just burn the cookie."

"That's where I challenge *you*, J," countered Azzie, resting his hand on Josh's shoulder as if to cushion the blow. "You're still looking at the wrong recipe." Azzie tapped the Giving theme on the P-E-O grid still visible on the whiteboard. "Giving is a key ingredient of the recipe, man. But it's not *the* ingredient. Yet the more money a person has, the more we seem to focus on that one . . . basically overlooking the other ingredients."

Azzie crossed his arms, satisfied. "That's one bad cookie."

Josh was clearly returning to life. "So you're saying we shortchange Bob and his growth if all we see is dollar signs?"

Azzie nodded. "Bro needs a few more ingredients, maybe a little bit more heat, before he becomes a full-grown cookie."

"A 'full-grown cookie'?" smiled Josh. "Az, your cookie analogy officially just crumbled. But point taken. And you know what I think the Bob recipe needs? More personal relationships with these teens. And, he needs to see firsthand some real healing and redemption."

Az turned toward Josh. "Then why not challenge him to mentor Omar?"

Josh spun to face his partner. "Are you kidding, Az? Omar's a good kid and all, but Bob may bring out the assault in him!"

"Maybe, maybe not," replied Az in a singsong voice. "Jesus was known to take a few risks, too."

He's right, thought Josh. *I just hope he's more right than me.*

"So okaaaaaayyy," Josh said hesitantly, "I am really going to call Bob and ask him to mentor the very kid he called a lost cause earlier today."

"Bro, you don't look excited," Azzie teased. "Come on, man! This is God changing lives, and we're vesseling again!"

Vesseling, meddling, meddling, vesseling, thought Josh as he returned to his desk and speed dialed Bob's office from his cell phone. He assumed a serious pose as the secretary transferred him to Bob. When he finally hung up the phone several minutes later, his serious expression did not betray the result of the call.

"So, what did he say?" Azzie said, looking up from his own computer.

"He said people don't usually talk to him like that. He thought for sure I was going to apologize. I almost did. But I fought that urge."

"And?" Azzie almost implored Josh to get to the point.

"He's in."

"In?" repeated Azzie incredulously.

"In, baybee!" replied Josh, punctuating his expression with a fist pump. "I can't believe it. We're going to head over to Juvie to pick up Omar this afternoon. Bob said when he saw that these kids mattered more to me than his money, he was impressed. I guess I won't tell him it was an accident, eh?"

All Bob's message said was, "Meet me at the Coffee Hut," thought Josh. *Unlike Mr. Direct to be so cryptic.*

Josh ordered his grande half-caf nonfat latte with sugar free hazelnut without even looking up. He was about to walk off to secure a table when he heard, "Nice, J. Not even a nod?"

He looked up to see Omar behind the counter in a black apron. He was barely recognizable as the same kid he'd picked up at Juvie only a month ago.

"I see you already discovered what I was going to show you," Bob said as he walked up behind Josh.

"But how?" Josh stammered.

"I know the guy who owns the place—and I helped him set up an LLC a while back—owed me a favor. He says Omar is a model employee. Even asked me if I know anyone else who might need a job."

Omar joined in, "I get to work before school, when people really need their caffeine fix. And getting school credit too. B-diddy here worked it all out."

"B-diddy?" mused Josh.

"At your service," grinned Bob, even bowing a little. "Shall we have a seat?"

As Omar turned to the espresso machine he said, "I'll bring the drinks over. Usual, B-diddy?" He didn't wait for the answer.

"Josh, I've been thinking," Bob began, suddenly turning serious. "How many of the kids you work with need help getting jobs? Filling out applications? Making connections?"

Josh laughed. "How many don't? That'd be an easier question to answer, because the answer would be *zero*. They all need to find work. We have a few connections and have had some luck with a couple of grocery stores and stuff. But for someone with a record, like Omar? Other than the license plate factory, they're pretty much out of luck."

"You need to do more, Josh," replied Bob sternly. "I've seen what having a job is doing for Omar. I'd like to see more of these kids have an opportunity like that."

"Well," Josh steeled his nerves and mustered everything he could remember about the P-E-O material on the whiteboards, "what do *you* want to do to help make that happen?"

"Well, I have lots of connections." If Bob found the challenge intimidating, he showed no signs. "I know the business community. But these kids need new clothes for interviewing, they need to practice their interviewing skills, and they need help filling out the applications."

Josh calculated his next words carefully. "We do all of that as we can, Bob, but we haven't had the resources or the volunteers to make it work."

"If I gave $500 each month for the clothes and other expenses, could you find more people to help?" asked Bob.

"Doubtful. But I bet you could—other business associates who might give their time to interview, give their old ties, stuff like that."

What are you doing? He just offered you $6,000 a year for a jobs program.

A clearly amused Bob replied, "You just don't know when to say 'yes' do you?"

"Of course I'm delighted to accept your gift, Bob," replied Josh, leaning forward in his chair with a new seriousness. "But I don't want it to substitute for your ongoing involvement with these kids. Look what you did for Omar. That's had a far bigger impact than any amount of money you could give."

"A bigger impact, huh?" replied Bob reflectively, relaxing back into his chair. "On him or on me?"

"On both. That's the beauty of it."

Bob interjected his next thought. "So you're saying that if it were an either/or, you'd rather have me come down and do practice interviews with these kids than to give my money to enable you to run the program?"

"Yes," replied Josh more confidently than he felt.

"You drive a hard bargain, Josh. But, I'm in . . . on both counts."

Josh returned to his office and approached the whiteboard. He wrote:

> REMEMBER: *Raising money God's way is about growing the donor, not the bank account.*

Then he scribbled "Do not erase" below it, capped the pen, turned out the light, and headed home.

REMEMBER:
Raising money God's way
is about growing the donor,
not the bank account.

Do not erase

To Ponder

Review your "To Ponder" responses at the end of Chapter 7. Then consider these next steps.

1. Think about an encounter with a donor who gives (or could give) large financial gifts to your ministry. How did you describe your ministry to him or her? What questions did you ask about the donor's own views? What questions or statements did you leave out? How was the conversation different than the way you describe your ministry to those you serve? Like Josh, do you have both a "ministry mode" and a "fundraising mode"?

2. Look back at the opportunities you listed on your P-E-O chart. Think about a time you did P-E-O without even knowing it. When you helped someone take a step forward, what was the result? Is that person still connected with your ministry? Is he or she more deeply connected now?

3. Think of another donor who gives regular, medium-sized gifts. In what way(s) might you have shortchanged his or her growth in relation to your cause by focusing only or primarily on the financial component? In which of your previously defined

themes does the donor need the most growth? What next step will you take?

4. Think again about a donor who gives (or could give) large financial gifts. What could you challenge that donor to do (or what belief or opinion could you challenge them to re-examine) that could deepen his or her involvement in your cause? In which of your previously defined themes does the donor need the most growth?

5. If your major donor strategy was a recipe, what ingredient do you think you've added too much of? What ingredients or steps are underrepresented or absent altogether?

Chapter 9

"**W**hat's up coach? You seem more energetic this morning. Go for a run?" Azzie inquired as Josh nearly bounded into the office.

"Better! I actually had my quiet time. Remember when we decided that we needed to challenge Lois to tackle some of the relationships in her family?"

Azzie faked an indignant look. "You mean do *I* remember telling *you* that's what we should do? Absolutely!"

"Well, God reminded me of it this morning. I really do think she's been using LLF to avoid those relationships. It's as though she feels the need to pay penance for how her children turned out. I was really convicted our job is to help release her from that guilt and try to minister to her own family."

Azzie nodded. "I think that's true. She's hurting, but she doesn't show it. She just works tirelessly as though she thinks she deserves every paper cut."

Josh kept going. "I also got another word today. Remember how we said O's still need to grow and be challenged? And remember that we're O's too, right?"

"Yep. I'm a cookie, you're a cookie, she's a cookie . . . wouldn't you like to be a cookie?"

"Well, even though we're LLF employees, we're first and foremost champions of this cause. And as champions, our primary job is to coach other champions."

Josh rapped his knuckles on the desk. "So here's the deal: I think God gave *you* the insight about where Lois needed some help to grow. So I think it should be you who talks to her."

Azzie looked genuinely startled. "Me? I'm only here for the food, J! I mean, I'm happy to do the books and stuff and work with teens, but I'm a better observer and critic when it comes to working with donors—er, champions."

"I know you don't do this job for the money, Az," affirmed Josh. "You love this ministry, this neighborhood, and these kids. And you're like a brother to me. But it's my job to challenge *you*, too. And you keep suggesting what I need to do. God has given you some amazing insight that has challenged me. Now it's my turn to turn it right back onto you."

Josh continued: "By being the one to talk to Lois, I think you will take a step toward greater ownership of this cause. Wouldn't you agree?"

Azzie whistled quietly. "Dang, J. That's a real stretch for me. Can I really tell our best champion that she has some growing up to do?" He exhaled. "But as Shakespeare said, 'Cowards die many times before their deaths.' How do you think she'll take it from me?"

"Probably better than she would from me, actually," assured Josh. "You can speak to her as a person who has been there. Tell her about your mom."

He gestured to Azzie. "Come on, Az—let's pray and then talk strategy."

"I could use the prayer . . . and some guts," replied Azzie, bowing his head.

"Did you see the fresh gang tagging at the park on your way over?" Lois inquired as Azzie walked into the Coffee Hut. "Just got off the phone with Mary Ellen and she's already rallying our little gang to do a little tagging of our own—and clean it up."

Azzie chuckled to himself at the almost mischievous grin on Lois's face before replying. "That Mary Ellen has turned out to be quite the gang leader. There's far more to that lady than being the queen of the scotchmellow cookie."

"Indeed. What did you want to talk to me about, Azzie? You sounded so vague on the phone. Surprise party for Josh or something?" Lois asked.

"Not exactly, Lois. Did I ever tell you about my mom?"

"No, I don't think you did."

"Well, you know I was a little wild as a kid. Did a short stint in Juvie before I got straightened out. Well, my mom did the best she could for a while, but then she started drinking bad. I used to go to the grocery store, pay the bills, even make her coffee in the morning to try to get her out of bed. Never thought much of it."

Lois nodded, her eyes glistening around the edges. "That's a difficult road for a little boy."

"But when I got picked up for shoplifting instant coffee for her, she was too drunk to pick me up at the station. A social worker set me up with a foster family. I'd see my mom sometimes when she would clean up. But by the time she cleaned up for good, I was too angry and bitter to listen to her. There I was in Bible school and I was still avoiding a relationship with my mom.

"Then, Josh visited me at Moody and told me he'd ran into my mom at church. He challenged me to reconnect with her. My first thought was, 'No way. She's a mess. She abandoned me.' And deeper than that, I also felt guilty for being unable to help her. I was defensive at first, saying I had a right to be mad at my mom. But Josh reminded me that wasn't the point . . . that Jesus often taught us to behave exactly opposite the way society would say we had a right to act.

"Didn't talk to Josh for a week. But then I called my mom to wish her a happy Mother's Day. First time we had talked in over a year. Then slowly we began to reconnect. It wasn't some magic moment. It was just work. Now we have dinner together every week."

"That's great Azzie. I am so glad for you," Lois said hesitantly, not sure where Azzie was leading.

"Lois," exhaled Azzie, nervous but resolute. "You know how Josh challenged me to reconnect with my mom? Well . . . I think *I* need to challenge *you* to reconnect—with your kids. I got into helping kids with addictions, but I wouldn't deal with the effect my mom's addiction had in my own life."

Lois glanced out the window, blinked hard and reached up her sleeve to retrieve the Kleenex she always carried there.

"I am afraid you are working with LLF, in part, because of the guilt you feel over how your kids turned out," Azzie resumed. "But God doesn't want you to serve out of guilt, Lois. He wants to release you from that guilt. You were a good mom who did the best you could."

Lois sniffed and blinked fast, trying to hold back tears. "I tried, but I worked so much. Maybe that is why . . . "

"That's what I mean, Lois. I want to work with you to heal those relationships."

Lois's normally confident voice was shaky as she said, "I don't see how. Most of my kids and grandkids have had trouble with drugs. They've stolen from me, lied to me. You know I even turned a couple of them into the police. Don't think they'll ever forgive me for that."

"We don't have to fix everything overnight," Azzie assured her. "You only have to take one step. Let's find one area you can work on right now." He paused for a moment, thinking. "How about your youngest—Esther? How are things with her?"

"The only time I see Esther is when she needs money. She has a job, but not a good one. It looks like she's kicked her drug habit—for the time being. I don't have any extra money to help her. But she's worn out working to support those two kids."

Lois pursed her lips. "I hate that those kids are home by themselves most afternoons until well into the evening. I am worried they're going to get into trouble too. They're really my last chance."

"Well then, let's start there," Azzie affirmed, pointing at Lois. "Let's map out a plan to reconnect you with Esther and her kids . . . to do LLF's ministry with them."

Lois cocked her head to one side. "Ministry *with* them? What do you mean?"

"You know how we did all that stuff with P-E-O? Well we've been using that to develop individual plans to help our champions grow. In fact, that's why I'm talking to you today," he admitted, sheepishly.

"I told Josh that I thought this whole family thing was an area we could work on with you. And I'm in the same boat because Josh thought I needed to grow, too. That's why he thought I should be the one to talk to you."

Lois let out a little laugh as she dabbed her eyes with her Kleenex. "I never really expected you two kids to tell this old lady to grow up. That's a very unique way to run a ministry. So, how does that apply to Esther and her kids?"

"Well, we have lots of opportunities to connect with LLF. You helped us create that chart, remember?"

Lois nodded.

"Well, some of those opportunities could apply to Esther and her kids. How old is your granddaughter Alesha—14?"

"Just turned 15 a couple weeks ago."

"What is she into?"

"She's a real artist. And she does it with computers. What's that called?"

Azzie leaned back in his chair, looking up as he thought. "Graphic design. A graphic designer. Maybe she could be a guest designer for our next newsletter . . . that you are helping write. The designer we've been using has been having a harder time fitting in our stuff since he does it for free. You and Alesha could work on it together."

Lois began digging around in her purse for a pen and paper. "That would be fun. I think she would like that."

Azzie continued. "What could be the next step for Alesha after that?"

Lois started jotting notes. "Maybe she could get some other kids together to work on that mural Mary Ellen wants our gang to put up over on MLK Boulevard. We were thinking it would be neat if it were designed by the teens we work with—help them learn about turning their neighborhood around. Alesha could do a little research to help develop a theme—maybe look into some other neighborhood projects around the country where art was used to make a difference. She could also help coordinate with some other kids to help dream up the project. That would be an E step, right? She would move from Participation to Engagement."

"Right!" Azzie offered a fist bump, but Lois seemed puzzled by the gesture. "Uh, well, you're getting the hang of the P/E/O part, anyway," he mumbled.

"So what about Anthony? How old is he now?"

"He's almost 10. For starters, as a P, he could come with me to stuff the newsletters Alesha and I work on together. I may have to bribe him with ice cream, but he'd do it."

"What else is he into?" inquired Azzie.

"The boy eats, breathes, and dreams basketball. I gave him a basketball for Christmas last year and I think he literally sleeps with it."

"Some people just have it in their veins. You remember Pete Maravich—Pistol Pete? He used to dribble out the car window as his family drove to town. Let's see . . . " Azzie rubbed his chin thoughtfully. "Basketball . . . basketball . . . Hey, the little gang Derek is leading is working on a project on the basketball courts over on 82nd and Hart. Putting nets up on all the empty rims. Think Anthony would like to go along?"

"I do," Lois nodded. "I think he would like that. It would be good for him to be around guys like that. Derek could be a great influence on him."

Lois and Azzie continued mapping out plans for Alesha and Anthony until Lois's tears had reverted back to her usual smiles and self-assured demeanor. Then she stopped suddenly, straightened, and grabbed Azzie's hand. "Your mom must be so proud of you."

"You won't believe what just happened!" exclaimed Josh as Azzie returned to the office.

"Um, let's see . . . You just talked to Jean, and she agreed to help coordinate the banquet. Am I right?"

Josh was taken aback. "What? How?"

"Dude, I was just with Lois," Azzie explained, laughing. "She knows everything. I guess Jean must have mentioned the idea to her during cookie delivery."

"Ok, well," sputtered Josh, searching around for some news with which to stump his friend. "Did Lois tell you how Jean wants to totally change the banquet?

"No. Missed that."

"So Lois doesn't quite know everything," Josh smiled. *Or she does but likes to still let me think I'm in charge,* he chuckled to himself. "Jean challenged me to abandon the spaghetti dinner altogether. She wants people to experience this cause first-hand."

"What—hot dogs at Big Al's hot dog stand?" queried Azzie, only half-joking.

"Close. She wants to do a progressive dinner. We'll start out at one of the nice hotels on the Westside where we'll have salad. But then we'll bus people over to Juvie to have our main course with the teens there. Then, we'll head back here for dessert—cookies, of course. And—get this—she wants to give each of the attendees a roll of cookie dough, challenging them to bake a sheet of cookies for the following week." Josh grinned, shaking his head. "Not sure if it'll work, but Jean knows more about this stuff than I do. She challenged me to take this step."

"That sounds more expensive than a spaghetti dinner," mused Azzie. "How will we afford it?"

"Well, that's another cool thing," replied Josh, drumming his desk. "We're gonna work together to get it completely underwritten before it even happens. And the first stop on our sponsor recruitment tour is gonna be First Assembly. After all, they've hosted the spaghetti dinner for years. Maybe they'll sponsor this one."

Josh looked over at Azzie suddenly. "Hey, anyway—how'd it go with Lois?"

"It went well, yeah, I think," nodded Azzie. "We put that P-E-O stuff in action to get two of her grandkids involved. And I found you a new graphic designer to help with the next newsletter."

As Azzie recapped his meeting with Lois, Josh kept remembering the passage he read that morning from Timothy.

Josh gestured to all the whiteboards filled with their musings and scribbles from the past few months.

"That right there is the point of all of this. You took a step, which helped Lois take a step, which will help her grandkids take steps. It's like Paul said in 2 Timothy 2: 'And the things you have heard me say in the presence of many witnesses entrust to reliable men who will also be qualified to teach others.'"

"Listen to you. And you call me the Bible scholar?" Azzie retorted.

Josh pulled up the whiteboard filled with lines and arrows from the earliest discussion about donor networks. "We've seen this in action. Over and over. Bob connected us to Jean who is now getting her friends involved. Lois is now spreading our cause in her own family. And Omar, who Bob was mentoring, now helps him in the jobs programs. This stuff is everywhere and most of it we're not even doing. It's amazing!"

Azzie jumped in. "And what's cool is, some of this is going on and we don't even know about it. The relationship between our champions is almost as important as their relationship with LLF. Did you know Mary Ellen's gang is working on a mural project? I just found out about that today. Dope. man. It's like you wrote right there," said Azzie, pointing to the board marked "Do not erase": "*Raising money God's way is about growing the donor, not the bank account.*"

"They're living out that Scripture where Jesus says, 'It is better to give than to receive.'"

Josh jumped up. "And that applies to us, too. I don't dread donor meetings as much any more, because I'm not asking them to sacrifice something to help LLF. I'm inviting them to join us on an adventure. *I'm* the one giving *them* something. And financial giving is a result of that, but not the only result."

Josh chuckled, shaking his head. "For years I complained about how donors weren't generous with us, or that they picked other charities.

But God is the God of abundance. There aren't limited resources. It was me doing it wrong—and thinking wrong. When we started being faithful to do things His way, He was true to his character."

"Yep," replied Azzie. "This whole conversation started months ago because we thought we needed more major donors. Turns out we *did* need them, but not the kind we thought. The real transformation happened when we stopped putting donors in categories by the size of check they write, and started categorizing them by their level of involvement with the cause—helping teens in this neighborhood."

"Absolutely true, Az," Josh agreed. "We knew we were asking for money wrong, but we thought it was just a matter of technique. We were assuming people wanted to give, and we just had to convince them to give to us. But really, a big part of our job is to teach them to give."

"Yeah—I was thinking about that on the way over here," added Azzie. "All this great stuff that has happened in the past few months— all of it originated from people we already knew. God had already given us all the champions we needed to grow this ministry. Now, we just need to follow this through, continue to grow our champions, and go through the doors God opens through them."

Josh gazed out the window in thought. "We're starting to see this work, Az. But man we messed up a few times along the way! Remember when I called Bob our 'real' major donor. Yikes!" Josh winced, then relaxed. "The cool thing is, now he *is* one of our real major donors. Totally invested. The money really has become secondary."

"Easy there, turbo," cautioned Azzie. "We still have a long way to go. It's not like we suddenly have more money than we know what to do with. And you'll probably still mess up a few more times when you stress out about meeting payroll. But we're on the right track."

Just then, they heard the front door to the office open and a quiet, "Hello?"

Josh walked into the entryway and recognized the woman from church, but didn't recall her name.

"Hey, I just had a baby girl a few months ago," the woman began hesitantly, "and I have all these extra baby clothes she's outgrown. Some of them have never even been worn. My friend Katherine sent me over. I guess her son Azzie works here. I wondered if you might know of a teen mom or someone with a little girl who could use them. Do you do that sort of thing?"

We do now, thought Josh.

"Absolutely," Josh said warmly. "In fact, we're having a baby shower next week for Claire, who's having a little girl in a few weeks. She needs all kinds of things. Hey, let me ask you something," Josh walked over to her with a glint in his eye. "Instead of dropping those clothes off now, how would you feel about bringing these things to her at the shower? The clothes would be a huge help, but what would be even more valuable to her would be to have another new mom there to help give her advice."

"That would be really cool," the woman replied, turning it over in her mind. "I may even have some more stuff I could bring for her. Maybe Katherine could come too. What else does she need?"

"Well," said Josh, fishing around for a piece of paper and a pen, "Let me connect you with Mary Ellen, who coordinates our baby shower program. She's the one who will know what Claire might need. What's the best way for her to reach you—phone, e-mail? I'm Josh, by the way," he said, extending his hand with the pen still in it, then awkwardly withdrew it, removed the pen, and then re-extended it.

"I'm Kelly," laughed the woman, "and e-mail would work best."

So this is how major donor development works! Welcome to LLF, Kelly.

To Ponder

1. Remember a time when you felt God gave you guidance or inspiration about your ministry. Did you listen and follow through? What was the result? How has that moment impacted your ministry?

2. Think of one of the best champions of your cause. In what category could he or she grow most? Like Azzie's step was to help Lois take a step, is there a way your champion could take a step that would help someone else take a step toward greater ownership of your cause?

3. Alesha is a teen that could be served by LLF, yet Azzie and Lois work to get her involved in doing the ministry with them. Think about a person your ministry serves or has served. Is there a way to get him or her involved in actually doing your ministry now? What is a step he or she could take at the P level? The E level?

4. Has there been a time when you discovered your champions were doing something for your ministry that you were unaware of (like Mary Ellen's gang and their mural)? If yes, how did you

react to the news? Were you pleased or worried? If no, how do you think you would react? How should you react?

5. Meditate on what Azzie said: *God had already given us all the champions we needed to grow this ministry. Now, we just need to follow this through, continue to grow our champions, and go through the doors God opens through them.* Do you believe that to be true? If that is true, what can or should be different about the way you communicate with your champions? About what you challenge them to do?

Making It Real

What? No million dollar check from Bob dropped by the office as the curtain drops on our novella?

No discovery that Lois is secretly a wealthy widow, so moved by Josh and Azzie's concern that she drops a million dollar check by the office (that lands right on top of Bob's million dollar check)?

No Azzie greeting Josh with a smile, brandishing a fistful of checks that just arrived in the mail as he says, "See, Josh? As long as we make the need known, we don't need to ask anybody for money. As long as we pray, God will put it on the hearts of good people everywhere to support this ministry"?

Nope.

Why?

Because Transformational Giving is about something much bigger than money changing hands.

That's the night-and-day difference between coaching champions and soliciting major donors.

In the traditional system of major donor identification, cultivation, solicitation, and affirmation, at the end of the day, the effort is viewed as successful if the organization's budget goals are met. Some major donors may give, some major donors may not, but as long as the funding gas gauge reads "Full," there are high fives and smiles all around.

Not so with Transformational Giving.

When we coach champions to give transformationally, we're making a commitment to measure and value three things above the size of our organization. We're making a commitment to measure and value:

Transformation in the *cause* on which our organization is focused.
Transformation in the *champions* which God has sent us to coach.
Transformation in the *coach*—namely, you!

To paraphrase Jesus' words in Matthew 6:33: Seek first to transform your *cause*, your *champions*, and your *self* . . . and your organization will grow in *all* the ways that truly matter.

I recognize that I'm committing fundraising "heresy" by sharing these thoughts with you. And as you read what I've written, you may be thinking, "Well, *yeah*, Eric, but let's be practical here . . ."

Yes. Let's!

Eric's Story

In the beginning of my fundraising career in the early 1990s, I worked with rescue missions. At that time, missions were absolutely exploding with growth due to some very successful fundraising techniques developed by ad agencies and fundraising consultants and mission fundraisers themselves.

More than a dozen missions literally went from five-figure budgets to seven- and eight-figure budgets in a decade's time. Gorgeous new buildings were being built. More meals were being served than ever. Missions were providing more nights of shelter, more shaves, more showers, more rehab programs, more Gospel services, more *everything* than they ever could have dreamed possible.

You can bet there were a lot of high-fives going around!

During that time period, I resigned my position as Vice President of the ad agency with the largest fundraising program for rescue missions in order to accept the position of President with the largest rescue mission in the United States. As I began to work directly with donors and foundations and the media in the daily effort to raise funds to support our mammoth (and expanding) budget, I found myself trumpeting our organizational *outputs*: number of meals provided, number of nights of shelter provided, number of this, number of that.

Then one day, I was talking to my father on the phone. He asked me a troubling question. "If your rescue mission closed today," he queried, "who would notice?"

At first, I was flabbergasted. Wasn't the answer obvious? We were one of the largest social service providers in one of the largest cities in America! Think of the meals that wouldn't be served if we weren't around . . . the beds that wouldn't be available for homeless people needing a place to sleep . . . the shaves . . . the showers . . . the rehab programs!

But the more I thought about my father's question, the less obvious the answer became.

I had always assumed that if the rescue mission was getting bigger and our programs were well conceived and executed and we were maintaining a healthy cost of fundraising along the way, well, then we *must* be impacting the cause . . . right? I mean, the cause of eradicating homelessness *must* be advancing if we're doing more . . . right?

I began to do some basic research into the numbers related to homelessness in our city. What I found blew me away. Despite our size, our growth, our generosity in helping other rescue missions in our city and around the country copy our approach and grow as well, there was *no discernable impact* on the statistics where I would have expected us to be making at least *some* kind of difference. My initial reaction was defensiveness. I protested to myself, "Well, the problem is just so *big*, you know. We can do only what we can do." And then I encouraged myself by saying, "If we help *even one person* . . . ." I probably would still be repeating those mantras to myself if it wasn't for the mission's major donors. What I found when I talked to them individually was that our marketing and fundraising efforts had fundamentally convinced them of something extremely alarming, namely, that *it was the mission's job to help the homeless.* Their job? To support the mission as they were able.

It was a recipe for fundraising success, that's for sure. It kept the funding tank on "Full" most of the time. The problem was, it wasn't a very biblical proposition. The Bible seems to maintain the attitude that it's the job of *each* person of faith to care personally for the poor. Through our marketing and fundraising efforts, we had professionalized individual biblical responsibility right out of existence.

Sure, we had a robust volunteer program. But it wasn't anywhere near as robust as the fundraising program where we convinced donors that helping the homeless principally meant sending in a check as often as they were able for as much as they were able.

The more research I did, the more I began to recognize that the problem wasn't unique to rescue missions. In fact, it may be the single most urgent issue facing Christian ministries in general in our time.

I urge you: take some time to do research like this yourself—for your own cause and for other causes that interest you.

» Does the rate of starvation drop in countries as the rate of child sponsorship in that country rises?

» Does the percentage of people professing faith in Jesus Christ go up in countries as more missionaries are sent there?

» As the number of Christian nonprofit organizations in the United States continues to increase exponentially, and as these organizations post larger revenue totals year after year, are American Christians becoming more generous with their income?

The answers seem obvious. To ask such questions even sounds foolish. But please, take time to research the answers for yourself.

You may end up having one of those transformational experiences that Josh and Azzie talk about with Bob, Lois, and Jean.

In my own case, my initial experience was anything but transformative. In truth, it was deeply depressing!

As a professional fundraiser, I'd always believed that the more money I raised, the more good was accomplished. Once that motivation was knocked out from underneath me, I had to ask myself: What's the point in raising money at all?

Enter the major donor. They're changing, you know.

Here's the fascinating thing about major donors: Their *natural* way of thinking is to be cause-driven, not organizationally-driven. That is, they don't initially get revved up about Live Life Fully, or XYZ Rescue Mission, or ABC Child Sponsorship Agency. They get revved up about helping wayward teens, caring for homeless people, and making sure kids around the world can grow up into adults around the world. *We're* the ones that convince them—through relentless solicitation by phone, mail, air, email, and birthday card—that *their* role is to support *us* as *we* solve these problems through our organization's ever-expanding programs.

We *used* to be able to convince them, anyway. On a number of counts, however, that traditional fundraising arrangement is falling apart.

For one thing, "donors"—especially major donors—are gradually rejecting the game by rejecting their role in it. Try to find a single commentator who contends that Christian giving as a percentage of individual income is trending upward. Be prepared: It'll be a long search. The unarguable consensus is that if Christian giving as a percentage of individual income is trending in any direction, it's not upward.

While it's popular to fault rank and file Christians for becoming more selfish over time, there's another way to read those statistics. The fact is, Christians are becoming less comfortable delegating the difference-making to churches and ministries who view the Christians' role in the process as serving as well-oiled ATM machines (why else do we call them "donors"?). Conversely, they are becoming more comfortable making a difference *themselves.*

Do some research into the amount of volunteer hours Christians are putting in around the country—not to mention around the world through the burgeoning short-term missions movement. Then study where the Millennial Generation turns when it wants to make a difference. It's not to us nonprofit organizations. It's to their far-flung network of friends on the Internet.

In my own journey, that's meant helping Christian non-profit organizations become the kind of places that could truly answer my father's searching question:

If your nonprofit organization closed its doors today, who would notice?

If you want to be successful in the future world of nonprofit fund-raising, the answer had better be:

All the champions who have networked together around our nonprofit and are being coached by us about how to personally impact the cause in accordance with biblical principles.

Do you think Lois and Bob and Jean and Kelly would notice if LLF closed its doors? You bet they would!

It's where they receive their training and where they carry out their ministry.

As a result, LLF's budget is *their* budget. Lois's budget. Bob's budget. Jean's budget. And soon, Kelly's budget.

They're not giving *to* LLF so that LLF can make a difference. They're personally making a difference in the cause *through* their service on behalf of LLF. In turn, LLF is coaching them on how to make an even bigger and more comprehensive difference in the cause. How? By growing them in each aspect of giving.

Between those two perspectives is a world of difference.

Look at where LLF is when the book ends: not quite flush with cash, and yet something has definitely changed in the character of the organization and the quality of the relationships within it. Josh and Azzie's words have changed, too, reflecting a change in their heart. They're still taking two steps forward and one backward—occasionally lapsing into old ways of thinking about God and money and major donors and the purpose of nonprofit organizations. But even their tentative Portland Two-Step has already resulted in four new champions being progressively unleashed for the Kingdom.

"But that would involve changing more than just our approach to major donor fundraising," you may be saying. "That would change the very nature of our nonprofit organization."

You're exactly right!

Start Slowly, Step by Step

Apply this book to your own situation and you'll find yourself on a transformative P-E-O journey of your own. And here's the best advice I can give you as a fellow traveler:

Don't start with a strategic planning meeting to discuss all this.

Don't begin by hashing it all out in a board meeting.

And definitely don't begin by being so overwhelmed by it all that you just set this book aside and feel paralyzed.

To paraphrase Azzie in Chapter 6, you don't have to begin with a perfect champion coaching strategy, man. All you have to do is help one champion move one step farther along the road.

My advice? Begin the way Josh and Azzie did: Stop seeking appointments with high rollers who couldn't care less about your cause. Stop defining a major donor as someone who gave (or could give) you single gifts of $1,000 or greater.

Instead, sit down with the Lois in your ministry. She is the one who gives a proportionally high percentage of her income to your ministry, whether that dollar amount is large or small. She doesn't just give *or* volunteer, but does both—and instinctively sees the value in each. She always seems to drag others along with her when she comes to your events.

When you sit down with your Lois, honor her passion and commitment to the cause, not your organization. Call her a champion, not a volunteer or a donor. Commit to being her coach. Let her know that you want to help her increase the impact she can have on the cause you both treasure. Support her instead of her supporting you. And use the tools in this book to help you do just that!

Five Transformational Steps

Here are the five transformational steps that, by the grace of God, will take you from soliciting major donors to coaching champions in your own organization:

1. Commit to tracking transformation

When the data we track doesn't match the data God tracks, our purposes won't match God's purposes. And let's face it: our major donor databases are built and organized primarily to track financial transactions. Our definition of who qualifies as "major" is a financial definition. And our definition of success has centered around keeping the funding tank on "Full." Does that sound like a system God would want to bless?

God keeps data for our sakes, not His. Likewise, when we commit to transitioning from soliciting major donors to coaching champions, we need to keep data for *their* sakes—so we can facilitate *their* growth, not simply the growth of our organization.

Ever think of your database as something that you would *want* to regularly share with those whose information is recorded in it? Almost as if it were a scrapbook or a photo album? That's what we're going to want to do with our champions as we track their transformation.

In *Revolution*, George Barna defined transformation as "Any significant and lasting transition in your life wherein you switch from one substantial perspective or practice to something wholly different that genuinely alters you at a basic level."

For our champions, we'll want to track one particular slice of that, namely, significant and lasting transitions in their life that relate to the cause you *both* hold dear—like inner-city youth work in the case of LLF.

It's important to remember that a significant or lasting transition in the life of your champion *ought* to include a record of their giving—if you're asking in a way that's designed to promote transformation, that is! If you're asking in a way that's designed to promote transformation, then you need to be recording more than just the gift date and amount. What transformation does the gift represent? A new insight into the cause? A new level of personal involvement? A more radical level of personal giving? If you record only the date and dollar amount, you'll never know.

Think about Bob's monthly giving commitment. In most ministry databases it would have been unceremoniously recorded as twelve $500 gifts, yet it represented an infinitely greater transformation in Bob's life. With monthly gifts, a new transformation might not be detectable each time the calendar page turns, but it sure ought to be detectable each time you get a new calendar. And the nature of that transformation ought to be something you're discussing openly with the champion himself or herself.

I'll have some tips for you on how to record transformational data in your champion database in a couple of page. Before that, however, we need to identify your ministry's specific transformational categories.

2. *Reverse engineer yourself*

What is the scriptural way of building a development program that enables champions to grow into the full stature of Jesus Christ?

Reverse engineering!

Think of it like this: You may be the greatest champion the Lord has gifted to your organization at present. How do you make more champions? Easy. Simply get your growing champions to imitate *you*.

Imitating anyone or anything typically draws lawsuits more than praise in individualistic Western culture. It sure draws a lot of kudos, however, if you read the New Testament. In 1 Corinthians 11:1, Paul writes, "Imitate me, just as I also imitate Christ," and in 2 Thessalonians 3:7, he adds, "For you yourselves know how you ought to follow our example." And it doesn't get much clearer than Hebrews 13:7, "Remember your leaders, who spoke the word of God to you. Consider the outcome of their way of life and imitate their faith."

This led Josh and Azzie to ask, "How'd I get here, anyway?" In other words, what were the transformational points in their lives that the Spirit used to grow them step by step into youth champions? This was a question they later took to Lois and also thought about in relation to Bob.

As our young heroes discovered, some of their steps were unique. Some were accidental. And some were errors that they wouldn't want anyone else to repeat!

But the more they thought about those transformational moments, and the more they talked to Lois and to Bob, they began to see patterns emerging that all the transformational moments had in common. Josh and Azzie were able to group into six categories the transformational moments that they had each grown through or were in the process of growing through on the way to full maturity in the LLF cause. Those six categories were: Relating, praying, serving, sharing, giving, and healing. They recognized that, in order to be a champion, an individual must be growing in *each category*, not just one or two. That's what led them to confront Lois, if you'll recall: the grid helped them to pinpoint the chink in Lois's armor, namely, she had not yet experienced transformation in the area of healing.

The categories that Josh and Azzie developed are good ones that could apply to just about any ministry. Still, they're best thought of only as a guide: your ministry should develop its own unique set. I've seen ministries effectively use as few as three and as many as ten categories, depending on their cause. The way to determine how many and which ones are necessary for your ministry is to ask, "What categories are *absolutely required* to form a fully mature champion for this cause?"

When Lois came along and re-drew those categories into a Participation/Engagement/Ownership grid, Josh and Azzie began to see that while each champion's journey is unique, the Holy Spirit does seem to have a sort of school by which He leads His people. Mostly, the

Spirit uses sensitive coaches like you to guide His champions step by step into the full stature of Jesus Christ in the cause you share.

Developing categories and creating a grid like this typically takes longer than it took Josh and Azzie. (Ah, the miracle of fiction!) It's no exaggeration to say that the answers you need will come only after prayer and fasting. It's also no exaggeration to say that the best way to begin is to prayerfully retrace *your* journey, just as Josh and Azzie did.

Now's the time to get out your own white board, or your prayer journal, or your Excel spreadsheet, and begin. Pray for the Holy Spirit to call to your memory each of the transformational moments through which He led you on your way to being the greatest champion for your cause. Of course, be prepared to write, cross out, get stumped, add, reword, combine, and produce several "final" drafts!

Not surprisingly, most of the ministries with whom I've worked through this process continually refine their categories *in cooperation with their champions.* Now *that's* transformational!

If you'd like a little practical inspiration before you begin, visit http://www.dare2share.org/map/ to see Dare2Share Ministries founder Greg Stier talk about the process as Dare2Share experienced it. You'll be able to download a copy of Dare2Share's own "MAP," or Mobilization Action Plan, which is the name they've given to their transformational data grid.

If you go to http://www.gregstier.org/mymap, you'll be able to see Greg's own personal MAP, regularly updated with the steps he sees God leading him through on the way to greater maturity in each of Dare2Share's categories. (Be sure to read the comments below Greg's post, as Dare2Share champions regularly post their own MAPs there, as well!)

3. Get your champions on the grid— and keep them on it until Jesus Christ returns

Throughout the book, you saw snippets and sketches of the transformational data grids that Josh and Azzie developed with or for their champions. Stop for a second and think what a transformational data grid is: it's a roadmap (MAP) to guide your champions to full maturity in Jesus Christ in relation to the cause you share.

The biggest mistake you can make once you develop that grid? *Failing to use it with every champion that God entrusts to your ministry.*

This is a recurring theme in the book. Josh and Azzie develop a transformational data grid for LLF. They celebrate it. They extol the wisdom in it. They show it to their champions. *And then they promptly fail to use it.*

You need to take your completed transformational data grid template and either photocopy 100 copies (there's something about this process that works well with pencil and paper) or save it over and over again on your computer, with each of your champions receiving their own file. Preferably in collaboration with each champion, complete a personalized grid for that champion for the next twelve months. If a champion is at the P level in a given category, work together prayerfully, just as Josh and Azzie did with their champions, to identify an E level goal. Then work together to equip them to grow into that goal over a specified time frame. If a champion is at the E level in a given category, brainstorm and set O level goals in that category. If a champion is strong in every category but one, of course, guess where you should help them focus?

Review a champion's grid with the champion regularly. I recommend monthly. Keep it updated. Encourage them to share it openly. Remember: Scripture calls on new champions to imitate mature champions! That can happen only if these plans are public.

Contrast this approach with the "moves management" process used by traditional fundraisers. There, "moves" are typically planned for a year as well. But these "moves" are planned by the fundraiser, not collaboratively with the major donor. And they're planned in private. And the moves are designed to ready the major donor to make a gift—things like "go fishing together," "send a birthday card," and "drop by donor's office." These are not Participation/Engagement/Ownership steps designed to grow champions who are having a progressively greater impact on the cause you both treasure. Instead, they're merely "plumping" steps to ready the turkey for Thanksgiving dinner!

Can you imagine if a major donor ever saw the plan drawn up by the fundraiser to "move" him or her to make a gift? Do you suppose seeing that plan would make the major donor more or less likely to give?

Now, think about how Josh and Azzie employed the grids they developed. Open. Transparent. Like a coach diagramming a play on a chalkboard—only in this case the coach and the quarterback create the playbook together, drawing upon the wisdom of the other coaches and quarterbacks that have come before them.

Don't feel pressure—and don't cause your champions to feel pressure—to grow in every category every month, or to become an O in every category by the end of Year 1. That would be impossible—real

Christian maturity takes *time*. Notice how Josh and Azzie worked with their champions to focus on specific areas. You can do the same, rotating between areas of focus each quarter or each year. Just remember: don't determine your focus on the basis of the champion's preference. Lois would never have agreed to focus on healing had it not been for Azzie's insistence.

And remember: your relationships with your champions should always be primarily characterized as mutual accountability relationships, not friendships or need-based hit-and-runs. This doesn't mean that you won't be friends with your champions, nor does it mean that you won't share with them needs that are appropriate for them to meet given the goals you've set together. It does mean, however, that those dimensions of your relationship will take place within a wider context.

That wider context is your accountability to God to coach the champions He sends you, and your accountability to the champion to equip them to grow in the ways God is calling them to grow (rather than simply the ways that they prefer).

4.   Recruit prospective champions, not new names for the mailing list

In traditional fundraising, ministries almost always make the same fundamental, cancerous errors.

Because they're trained to think in terms of donors rather than champions, and because they typically have to cull through loads of "regular" donors in order to find a "major donor prospect," they're convinced they need to gather as many names as possible. So executive directors pass around a signup sheet when speaking at churches and rent lists of names to which they then send out acquisition snail- and e-mail. Respondents are dumped into the ministry's mail stream, from which potential major donors are thought to eventually bubble to the top.

Big mistakes at every turn.

Champions may *survive* traditional mass fundraising programs and thus draw your attention to them, like strong salmon swimming upstream. But traditional mass fundraising programs blatantly ignore the scriptural truth that giving is learned, not latent. This is a trustworthy saying that deserves full acceptance: The Christian ministry future belongs to organizations committed to recruiting champions, not those focused on building donor files. A few well-coached champions will outperform hundreds of donor solicitation prospects any day of the week.

The other mistake ministries make in traditional fundraising is to spend staggering amounts of time courting individuals who have the capacity to give . . . but who don't have the slightest inclination to become champions of your cause. This is the trap Josh has fallen into as the book opens, doing lunch after lunch with "high net worth" individuals.

Thankfully, Lois gently guides Josh through the process of understanding why this practice is theologically repugnant. In addition, there are many nuts and bolts reasons why this is bad time management. Do the math yourself:

You can spend months pursuing a "tease"—someone who could make a very large gift, but who never does. Or . . .

You can immediately equip someone to mobilize his or her entire network of friends, such as Lois did with her cookie companions. By the end of the book, Lois is coaching her own champion, Mary Ellen. No ministry lunches or birthday cards required. And not just because she's a "low net worth" individual (try using that phrase with the Lord when you stand before the Great White Throne, by the way).

As you work with champions, it's important to keep the Participation/Engagement/Ownership framework in mind. Champions typically won't be ready to think about completing a personalized transformation grid with you until they reach the E level in at least two or three areas. In fact, creating a personalized grid together with you is in itself a great coaching "move" for a maturing champion.

Think of how this focus on transformational data can begin to change the way you relate to and recruit potential champions.

First, as you meet people, you'll now have a set of cause-oriented champion-building questions in your mind that go beyond, "So how long have you gone to church here?" In Josh's case, for example, he can ask, "What experiences with youth have been the most transformational ones for you so far?" The reply to his question—which could be anything from a blank stare to a clarifying question to an angry rant to a tearful recollection—can be run through the LLF transformational data grid in Josh's mind. Sometimes he'll know immediately how to respond. Sometimes he won't. But the more he does this kind of thing, the better he'll get at being able to invite even "pre-P's" (those who have no prior connection to the cause at all) to participate in a particular project that he discerns will start their journey toward championhood.

Not coincidentally, *Jesus* happened to be an expert at that very thing!

Second, as you converse with your maturing champions about the cause-related transformations they've experienced and are experiencing, you'll gradually be building *transformational relationships*. These won't be relationships built on remembering major donors' birthdates or knowing secret information about their liquidity. They'll be relationships in which you're acknowledging, encouraging, and furthering the donor's growth in the cause, in concert with the Holy Spirit.

Third, think about how much more productive you will be in talking to your champions specifically about their financial giving. Instead of hemming and hawing around, feeling generally yucky as you try to look for an opening to blurt out your organization's financial need, you can decide which opportunities to present (and not present) depending upon what you have learned about the champion's previous experiences in giving to your cause.

And with champions who are "on the grid" with you, you'll have already set goals together. Therefore, your ask will be in response to the goals the two of you have already written down. Imagine that!

5. Track transformational data in such a way that you can act on it

Moving from major donor solicitation to coaching champions means more than changing the way you make notes in the "Comments" section of your individual donor records. That's because instead of choosing who to mail or contact based on the timeliness, frequency, and amounts of a person's gifts, you will select specific champions to receive certain messages (through the mail, via email, and when you meet in person).

You'll make those decisions based on what next steps are logical given the transformations they've experienced to date and the ones they're most likely to experience next.

Building a database sounds exceedingly technical, and in some ways it is. But everything discussed in this book is easily accomplished using a Microsoft Excel spreadsheet—Azzie's database of choice. Thankfully, every major database product on the market today can be tweaked to do, to greater or lesser degree, what I'm proposing here. That's because we're simply recording more data (not just financial transactions) in such a way that it can be searched or selected as the basis for a communication with certain select champions.

Here's a summary of the steps you'll need to follow:

First, finalize the list of common steps your champions will pass through on the way to full maturity. Don't pressure yourself to try to put them in a specific sequence. After all, spiritual growth rarely follows the same linear pattern for everyone. But do group them in categories, and think through which steps might fit each category at the Participation, Engagement, and Ownership levels of the champion maturation process. Then create a list of every possible transformational action step. For LLF, for example, that would include things like making cookies, leading a gang, and working personally with a troubled teen.

Second, convert this list into a set of short statements that can be checked or unchecked in a donor record: "Champion has participated in a cookie distribution" or "Champion is engaged in a gang" or "Champion has worked personally with a troubled teen." That kind of binary yes/no, on/off, selected/unselected form of recordkeeping will make it easy for you to use the data to segment your champions for mailings, e-mails, and personal communications. This also has the advantage of being easy enough for even the smallest ministry to do using a program like Excel. And if you're using a formal database already, you'll be able to transition from donor solicitation to coaching champions without tossing your existing record structure out the window.

Third, transformational data deserves to be shared and remembered. Your database needs to be a transformation scrapbook, not a fancy cash register. Create space in each champion's record to note their transformations in more detail. You won't be using these entries to search on, of course, but they will prove immensely helpful to you and others in your organization whenever you need to refresh yourself on a particular champion's journey.

Fourth, don't forget to train your staff and data entry operators to track transformation, not just transactions! It'll take everyone a while to get used to the idea that the database is more than a list of gifts. Share this book with them. Once you create your transformational data grid, and once you make it possible to keep track of each champion's progress along that grid, encourage and exhort each other regularly to record the transformations your champions are experiencing.

Notice that Josh and Azzie served as mutual accountability partners in this regard. They nudged each other to create personalized grids for each champion. They talked regularly, celebrated victories, and even worried a bit about each of the steps their champions were taking—both forward and backward. You can almost hear Paul in Galatians 4:19 as he groans, "My dear children, for whom I am again in the pains of childbirth until Christ is formed in you . . ." Ask the Lord to give you lots of grace every step along the way.

There's More!

You and I may not work in the same office like Josh and Azzie, but our need for mutual accountability and encouragement as we (a) stop soliciting donors and (b) start coaching champions is no less crucial. That's why I want to invite you to visit my blog at **http://coachyourchampions.com**. There you'll find:

✎ My real-life experiences in coaching champions and equipping ministries to coach their own champions

✎ Sample transformational data grids for champions from ministries applying the principles in this book

✎ Free video clips from Mission Increase Foundation workshops and labs

✎ A link to a list of upcoming Mission Increase Foundation training events in your area

✎ Ongoing counsel on how to apply the Transformational Giving Ten principles to the rest of your fundraising program

✎ My ongoing comments on blogs, articles, and books of interest to individuals who like the kind of thinking you've run into in this book

You can post your own comments on the blog, too. I'd love to hear them! It matters supremely to me that you feel supported and encouraged as you begin to put into practice the things you've read here.

As we say when we end each Mission Increase training event, "*You can do this.*"

After all, the Holy Spirit, your own Lois(es), MIF, and I are all here to help!

Annual Champion Coaching Plan

Relating	Action	
	Result	
Praying	Action	
	Result	
Serving	Action	
	Result	
Sharing	Action	
	Result	
Giving	Action	
	Result	
Healing	Action	
	Result	

Annual Champion Coaching Plan

Relating	Action	
	Result	
Praying	Action	
	Result	
Serving	Action	
	Result	
Sharing	Action	
	Result	
Giving	Action	
	Result	
Healing	Action	
	Result	

Annual Champion Coaching Plan

	P		E		O	
	Action	Result	Action	Result	Action	Result
Relating						
Praying	Action	Result	Action	Result	Action	Result
Serving	Action	Result	Action	Result	Action	Result
Sharing	Action	Result	Action	Result	Action	Result
Giving	Action	Result	Action	Result	Action	Result
Healing	Action	Result	Action	Result	Action	Result

Annual Champion Coaching Plan

	P		E		O	
Relating	Action	Result	Action	Result	Action	Result
Praying	Action	Result	Action	Result	Action	Result
Serving	Action	Result	Action	Result	Action	Result
Sharing	Action	Result	Action	Result	Action	Result
Giving	Action	Result	Action	Result	Action	Result
Healing	Action	Result	Action	Result	Action	Result

Acknowledgments

The best insight I ever received into major donor development and the coaching of champions came from my wife, Hyun Sook. "Food," she said, "does not come in a box." We were not at that moment talking about major donor development or the coaching of champions. Nor were we at that moment married. Rather, we were engaged, and she was visiting my townhome and taking an astonished inventory of my pantry, which, as you can now surmise by her comment, consisted entirely of foods in boxes and wrappers—freeze-dried noodles of this kind and TV dinners of that kind, Library of Congress-sized stacks of ramen noodles, and more jars of peanut butter than are stocked in the pantries of my Mormon friends.

The only thing in my whole house that passed the "Food" test was a single watermelon that she had bought me a week or two earlier, which I had not yet touched because, I reasoned, it was too large to fit in the microwave, the one food preparation apparatus I was able to successfully operate.

I am happy to report that not only are we sublimely happily married and more so with each passing year, and not only do I now eat healthier than cheetahs in the wild thanks to my wife's peerless care, but I learned lessons about major donor development and the coaching of champions from this godly companion that I simply could have never learned anywhere else.

Namely: If food doesn't come in a box, donors sure don't either.

Instead, donors are Holy Spirit-built, not nonprofit-discovered; they're invited, coached, and challenged, not solicited; they're savored with our full attention, not wolfed down in five minutes while we are busy doing other things.

I am also permanently and affectionately a debtor to the Christian ministries who have not only extended to me unconditional trust to raid their donor pantries and prepare development meals, but who have dramatically improved the quality of my cooking over the years by joining me in the kitchen: Fred Palmerton at Christian Resources International; Cavin Harper at Christian Grandparenting Network;

Laura Baker at Prasso Ministries; Ali Eastburn at With This Ring; Matt Dubois at .W; Tim Rickel and the gang at World Gospel Mission; Greg Stier, Debb Bresina, and Dave Teraberry at Dare2Share Ministries. The ministry to champions we've done together bleeds onto every page of this book, as does that of my wife's own organization, Seoul USA. These are great ministries not only because their causes are Kingdom critical and their organizations well run; these are great ministries also because they are continually unleashing a vibrant new crop of champions into the world.

Without Mission Increase Foundation's Rebekah Farquhar and Amy Karjala, aided by MIF's Matt Baxter and Tracy Nordyke, this book wouldn't be in your hands. They drafted sections of chapters, edited sections of chapters, brainstormed plot twists and, to paraphrase the writer of Hebrews, did the literary equivalent of turning to flight the armies of alien typos and schedule killers.

Without Mission Increase Foundation's Dave Farquhar, this would be a greatly impoverished book. The writer of Proverbs said, "How I hated discipline! How my heart spurned correction!" The writer of Proverbs apparently never got to work with Dave. Dave is a true Christian brother and a gifted coach. Most of the really good parts of the book are connected to him somehow. No small number of the really good parts of my life are connected to him, too.

It's impossible to write a book about coaching champions without thanking those who over the years have exemplified for me the journey from donor to champion: Dale and Gail Stockamp, Doc Haggstrom, Gary and Bev Forrest, Stephen Garner, Bob Faulkner, Jerry and Debbie Kidwell, John and Nancy DeMund, Phil and Bev Simpson, and Alan and Dolores Hardin. Alan was the first champion ever to rebuke me, as we sat in his hot tub during a visit I was honored to pay to their home years ago. "Eric," noted Alan, "you have all the marks of a man who is rejecting the calling of God upon his life." Alan, you were right. I submit this book as token of my repentance and gratitude.

Finally, I thank the Lord for bringing you and me together through this book, to the glory of His Son. I pray He uses this book to further His purposes in both of us.

About the Author

The Reverend Eric Foley is the Vice President of Training for Mission Increase Foundation. A much sought-after development and marketing consultant for nearly twenty years, Eric's work has encompassed a broad range of nonprofits including Promise Keepers, Voice of the Martyrs, the Los Angeles Mission, the LA Dream Center, and now nearly thirteen hundred other organizations through his monthly Mission Increase Foundation workshop training events. He is the co-founder with his wife, Hyun Sook, of Seoul USA, an organization devoted to building bridges of understanding between the Korean and American communities. The Foleys live in Colorado Springs, Colorado.

Rev. Eric Foley
Mission Increase Foundation Colorado
1155 Kelly Johnson Blvd., Suite 111
Colorado Springs, CO 80920
Office (719) 757-1123
Fax (719) 213-2595

About Mission Increase Foundation

Mission Increase Foundation believes there is a better way for ministries and donors to serve together. Every year billions of dollars are given to Christian charities, yet most donors do not believe they are being the good stewards God desires them to be. At the same time, despite all the giving, most nonprofit organizations still feel they lack the resources and skills needed to fulfill their missions.

As you've seen in this book, we teach a Transformational Giving model based on Scripture that has the power to transform both the giver and the recipient. Transformational Giving allows a caring donor's giving to build each ministry and impact the cause about which the ministry and the donor care deeply. Further, the ministry supports its donors by equipping them to grow into champions of the cause, rather than treating donors merely as supporters of the organization's own work.

Mission Increase Foundation is a private operating foundation whose goal is to transform lives for Jesus Christ by providing grants and training to local Christian ministries. We couple donors' giving with specialized training to ensure grant recipients have the tools they need to succeed. The combined power of specialized training and cash grants helps nonprofits grow and transform not only their communities, but also the hearts of their donors.

Currently we have offices in Colorado Springs, Denver, Los Angeles, Phoenix, Portland, San Francisco, Seattle, and Mexico City.

For more information on how you can become involved in Transformational Giving through Mission Increase Foundation, visit www.missionincrease.org or contact our national office:

Mission Increase Foundation
5665 SW Meadows Rd, Suite 160
Lake Oswego, OR 97035
Office (503) 639-7364
Fax (503) 210-0283

·

Made in the USA
Monee, IL
18 June 2020